# RELEASING GOD'S ANOINTING

by

Mel Bond

*His brightness was like the illumination of the morning sunlight with rays of sunlight splendor streaming out of His hands, and there in that sunlight splendor was the hiding place of His miracle-working power.*

*Habakkuk 3:4*

*As He is, so are we (that believe, trust, have faith and confidence) in this world.*

*I John 4:17*

All Scripture quotations in this volume are taken from the King James Version of the Bible and the Hebrew and Greek fuller meaning of words.

# CONTENTS

**Introduction**

# DEDICATION

*To Darlene and Richard March with great love and respect.  III John 2:4*

*Mel & Donna*

# INTRODUCTION

Jesus explained to me how to pray with my whole heart, so that others would receive instant healings and miracles every single time. This comes about through being single-minded, in order to release and receive God's anointing.

Unobvious demons are quite often, if not always, present to prevent Christians from being single-minded. These demons attempt to make you think you may not be praying correctly, or doubt whether the person you are praying for will be healed, or wonder what others will think about how you are ministering. These not-so-obvious demonic suggestions hinder God's anointing. A double-minded person will not receive anything from the Lord.

Jesus taught me that yielding to God is important in receiving, and it is as simple as physically relaxing. The word "yield" in the Greek means to relax or surrender. Romans 6:19 teaches that as we have yielded our members to sin (satan), we can yield our members to God's holiness. Holiness is God's reputation. We can simply relax and surrender to God's reputation being manifested in our mortal bodies. God has a reputation of the miraculous, and it is easier to yield to God's glory than it is to yield to sin, because God is greater than satan.

I have been filled with the Holy Spirit, with the evidence of speaking in tongues, since June 17, 1958. Since that time, I have prayed for many people while evangelizing, holding crusades and pastoring. I believed in healing and miracles, but had only experienced about 5 percent results, as years without instant manifestation passed by.   With Jesus' explanation of how to pray with my whole heart, I now know how to release God's anointing, and experience instant manifestation in about 90 percent of the people for whom I pray.

# CHAPTER 1

# THE VISION OF CHRIST

Before discussing Jesus' teaching on how to release God's anointing, I must emphasize that the Scripture is the final authority. In Psalm 138:2, God exalts and promotes His Word above all, even above Himself. 2 Corinthians 10:5 teaches that any thought, perception, imagination, reasoning, subject or discourse must be in obedience and subjection to Christ. According to John 1:1,14, all reasoning should agree with and obey the Word of God, as Christ and the Word of God are equal terms.

Furthermore, in Matthew 15:6, Jesus said that God's commandments are made none effective by traditions. This includes legends, religious customs, preconceived intellectual practices and man-made religious teachings. Above all, God's Word must always be put first. Paul said in Galatians 1:8, "But though we, or an angel from heaven, preach (teach or promote) any other gospel (than the Word of God), let them be accursed." Paul also said that satan has the ability to transform himself into an angel of light.

Visions and supernatural manifestations are to be judged according to the Word of God, in order to avoid deception. God's Word must always come first. I do not exalt any type of teaching, vision or manifestation of supernatural beings above the Word of God. I do not, however, want to void or belittle the sound doctrine of the visions of Jesus. John 14:21 says, "He (or she) that has My commandments and keeps them, it is that person that loves Me and he (or she) that loves Me shall be loved by the Father, and will manifest Myself to them." The Greek meaning of the word "manifest" is to exhibit in person, appear or show.

Anyone who has read the New Testament could safely assume that Paul loved Jesus more than any other person loved Jesus in the New Testament, as his writings bear proof. Also, more than any other person in the Bible, Paul loved the Word of God. He is responsible for writing nearly half of the New Testament through the inspiration of the Holy Spirit.

Valuable wisdom is found in many of Paul's experiences. In Galatians 1:12, Paul said that he was not taught the Word of God by man, but by revelation of Jesus Christ. In Galatians 2:1-2, Paul, Barnabas and Titus went to Jerusalem, but Paul went to Jerusalem by revelation. Galatians 1:12, 2:12, indicates that Paul went in person. The word "revelation" in the Greek means to appear, manifest or to be coming. In the King James Version of the Bible, the word used is "appearing".[1]

In 2 Corinthians 12:1, Paul talked about the revelations of the Lord, and in verse 7, he had an abundance of revelations. Again, the same root word for revelation or appearing is used. Continually, Jesus appeared to Paul and taught him the Word of God.

Jesus first appeared to Paul in Acts 9:4, and his life was forever changed. Paul even changed his own name. In

---

[1] Strong, James. *Strong's Exhaustive Concordance.* Massachusetts: Hendrickson Publishers, pg. 657.

8

verse 17, Jesus taught Paul by asking him why he persecuted Him. In Acts 18:6-11, an upset Paul made up his mind to change the course of his ministry, but Jesus appeared in a night vision and encouraged him to continue his ministry. Because of this vision, Paul continued in that city for a year and 6 months.

Acts 22:17-21 finds Paul in Jerusalem praying at the temple. As he prayed, he saw Jesus, Who told him to make haste and get out of Jerusalem, quickly, for the people there would not receive his ministry. Acts 23:11 gives yet another account of Jesus appearing to Paul in the night, giving him words of cheer, encouraging his ministry and telling Paul that he would be a witness in Rome.

In Acts 27:14-22, a great storm arose as Paul was on a ship bound for Rome. Neither the sun nor the stars appeared for many days, and all hope that any would be saved was lost. After a long period without food, Paul stood up in the midst of the men on the ship and exhorted them to be of good cheer. Acts 27:24 tells of an angel of God who stood by Paul that night, serving him and saying, "Fear not, Paul; thou must be brought before Caesar: and, lo, God hath given thee all that is with thee." "Wherefore, sirs, be of good cheer: for I believe God, that it shall be even as it was told me" (Acts 27:25).

Once again, Paul received instruction to encourage and strengthen him supernaturally, through the appearance of an angel sent from God. I believe there is a strong implication that it was Jesus who came to Paul in verse 25, when Paul says, "For I believe God." Regardless of whether or not it was Jesus or an angel who appeared before Paul, there was a supernatural, spiritual appearance that stood by Paul, and it was God-ordained. As you read this, a thought from satan may already be tempting you, saying that Paul was

9

special, or telling you that those things do not happen, today. There is Scripture that will destroy those thoughts. Hebrews 13:8 says that Jesus Christ is the same yesterday, today and forever. In the Word of God, Jesus has different names and according to Revelation 19:13, one of the names is the *Word of God*. Hebrews 13:8 clearly displays Jesus as never changing in doctrine, love or in the way in which He deals with humanity. This further supports that He appears to people, today.

Also, God does not just pick out certain people and say that they are to be His special chosen ones. 2 Chronicles 16:9 says, "The eyes of the Lord run to and fro over the whole earth to show Himself strong on the behalf of those whose heart is perfect toward Him." He isn't looking for someone who is perfect, but for someone whose heart is perfect.

He is looking for those who hunger and are open-minded towards God and the realm of the Spirit. In James 4:8, God says, "Draw nigh unto me and I will draw nigh unto you." He is giving all of humanity an invitation into His presence. In Psalm 37:4 He says, "Delight yourself in the Lord, and He will give you the desires of your heart."

God does not just choose certain people to be special. Rather, people choose God to be special to them. This is why I believe that the Lord appears to people, today. If you delight in the Lord, He will give you the desires of your heart.

It isn't because of my holiness that I have had visions. God makes the offer to all. You will notice this same type of offer in the following passages: Jeremiah 33:3, Jeremiah 29:13, Matthew 6:33, Psalm 34:10, Psalm 23:1, I John 5:14-15, Mark 11:24, Mark 9:23, Ecclesiastes 5:20 and

John 16:24. These are just a few of the many Scriptures that support the truth that God does not choose certain people in which to be special. Instead, people choose for God to be special to them, allowing Him to reveal Himself to them.

# THE VISION

On Friday evening, September 28, 1984, I had a vision. In the vision, I was preaching in the church I was then pastoring, and perceived that there was a woman in the service who needed healing in her body. In my vision, I called her to the front, and began to pray for her. When she came forward, I felt someone behind me put their hand on my right shoulder, and I turned to see who it was. It was the Lord Jesus Christ, the Son of God. Then Jesus described to me the woman's ailment and said, "Pray with your whole heart, and My anointing will go into her, and she will be healed."

If you have ever experienced the spirit realm, you know that when words are spoken, volumes of information are transmitted. Often times, lips do not move, audible words are not spoken, yet volumes of information are transmitted. The way that Jesus told me to pray in that vision is what this book is about.

On that very Sunday that followed the vision, I finished preaching and simply acted out what I had experienced in the vision. I called the woman forward, and asked her if what Jesus had told me about her physical need was correct. She admitted the same condition, so I ministered to her in the way that Jesus had explained, and she was instantly healed.

# PRAYING WITH YOUR WHOLE HEART

The instructions Jesus spoke to me during that vision were so simple. The more I meditate on the experience, the further I understand the knowledge that was transmitted in the realm of the Spirit. This is because when Jesus speaks, His words are alive and forever live. Anything that is alive must continue to grow, and God's words are more alive than anything else in existence. However, the only way His words can continue to grow in us is by meditating, thinking and giving those words a place in our lives.

There are several points to be made regarding Jesus' instruction about praying with your whole heart. Matthew 5:8 says, "Blessed are the pure in heart: for they shall see God." The Greek word for "see" in this passage is *op'tom'ahee*, which means to have a vision. As you study this passage, you will find that the word "heart" refers to the spirit, and there is only one way a person can have a pure, clean spirit, and that is through being born again.

It is simple to have your heart whole, clean and pure. If you are already born again, allow that Christ-like spirit that is within you to have its way, for your spirit is always willing and wanting to see God. It is your flesh that is weak and unable to see, comprehend or relate to the things of God. The things of God are of the Spirit world. Hebrews 10:21-22 says, "Let us draw near (to God) with a true heart."

God invites all of humanity to live in His presence. Simply learning to pray with your whole heart will allow you entrance into the very presence of God. In this Scripture, God says that we can draw near to Him with a true heart. If Jesus is the Lord of your life, you have a true, perfect heart or spirit. The greatest reason for learning to pray with your whole heart, as Jesus said, is so that anything you pray for will be instantly manifested.

Psalm 16:11 says, "Preserve me, O God: for in thee do I put my trust." In His presence, we are shown the path of life. There isn't an entity in existence that knows more about life at its best, fullest, most satisfying, most exciting and most complete, than God, Himself. Yes, there is pleasure in sin, but that pleasure is not as satisfying as God's pleasure, because satan's pleasure is counterfeit. In addition to being counterfeit, it will only last for a season, and then the wages of torment and destruction come.

Even if sin had no ill after-effect, it is of the devil, and the devil cannot out-do God on any account. If we give in to sin, we give in to the devil. The pleasures of God are always more fulfilling, satisfying and exciting than the pleasures of sin. If you have not yet found that out, get into God's presence and see for yourself.

In God's presence is direction from God, Himself, into this abundant life and fullness of joy. As you study *joy* in this passage of Scripture, you will find this is the same joy that God experiences. There isn't a fuller joy in existence than the joy that He experiences, and it can be yours by simply getting into God's presence. In His presence is pleasure, forevermore. Anything else is an extremely cheap imitation.

There was a time when my wife and I sold most of our possessions, walked away from our business and moved across the United States to pastor a small church of about 15 people. From a natural viewpoint, everything you can imagine went wrong, yet we were happy in our hearts.

One evening, I was awakened to the fullness of God's presence, as I had never experienced it before. When God wakes you up during the night session, you are more alert than you would be during the most alert time of your natural life. None of my natural sensibilities related to this experience, but the fullness of His person was manifested in ways that I had never known before.

The Lord spoke to me and said, "I love you so much, more than you could ever possibly imagine, and I am here to ask if there is anything I can do for you." The Lord was telling me that He would fulfill my needs, no matter what I requested. His presence was so awesome, beyond the human ability to understand. I simply wept and said, "Dear Lord, You are doing it." He was giving me more than anything this world could possibly even imagine, by simply being in my presence. Now, if this had happened during a time when my natural sensibilities were ruling, I would have given Him a long list of things that I thought were needs.

Although, it might not have been God's perfect will for us to pastor that small church, He instilled in our lives a supernatural foundation. The spiritual experiences occurred on a daily and sometimes hourly basis. And, although, we suffered tremendously in the natural realm, we prospered spiritually. To this day, I have not had the visions and spiritual experiences that I had during that time of our ministry.

God eventually paid us back in the natural, far beyond what we ever thought would happen in our lives. If your heart is right, God will even honor your mistakes. When your heart is right, I am not sure you can even make a mistake that won't work for your good in the end. God offers each of us a way of life that is supernatural, and all we have to do is learn to receive what has already been given to us.

2 Chronicles 16:9 says, "For the eyes of the Lord run to and fro through the whole earth, to show himself strong in the behalf of those whose heart is perfect toward Him." God isn't looking for people who have arrived at perfection, because there are none. He is looking for someone like Abraham, who was counted as perfect and righteous, because he believed God. God certainly did not choose Abraham because he had his natural life in order.

It is so simple to have a perfect heart. Man-made doctrines and doctrines of devils are difficult, but the doctrines of God are simple. Psalm 119:130 says, "The entrance of God's Words give light (direction); it gives understanding to the simple." God isn't in it, if it isn't simple.

Proverbs 23:7 teaches, "As a person thinks in their heart so are they." Your heart is your spirit, and the only way to think spiritually is with spiritual substance. There is nothing more pure and more perfect in spiritual substance than the eternal Word of God. So, think what God thinks and says about you.

The Scriptures tell us that we are as Holy as God. We have God's exact reputation. The Scripture says that God cannot find faults or failures in us. According to Colossians 1:22, we are holy, unblameable and unreproveable in His sight.

There are some who become angry at this message, because they feel as if they have to earn their holiness and righteousness. But I know that God's treasures are simply given to all who read the Word, believe It and act as if It is the truth. This Godly reputation is too pure, too holy and too good for any human to earn, so stop trying. This will only take you further away.

If God sees you differently, it makes no difference how anyone else thinks or sees you. I choose to believe God's report rather than the world's report. Deuteronomy 4:29 says, "If thou shalt seek (desire, require) the Lord thou shalt find Him, if thou shalt seek (frequently diligently, require) Him with all thy heart and with all thy soul." When we want God, to the degree that He is a requirement in our lives, we will find Him.

In natural life, we have major requirements that must be met in order to stay alive. We can only live a few minutes without air, only a few days without water, and only a little over a month without food. When God becomes as much of a requirement as food, water or air, then we will find Him.

Many years ago, a dear uncle of mine, Uncle Ben, lost his youngest son in a car accident. He told me about times he would go to bed and cry night after night, because he felt the great torment of deep sorrow. One night, he cried out to God like never before, "Dear God, I have to have help." He prayed in a whole-hearted fashion. He said that when he prayed like this, God gave him what he needed in the manifestation of a vision. From his description, I believe that my uncle was translated to heaven. The experience changed his life. The glory of God shone on his face, even after a year had passed. I believe that he had the same kind of experience that Moses had when he came into God's presence. The torment lifted from his life, and it became naturally visible that he had been transformed. The key to his revelation was found in his very words. He told me, "When I became serious with God, He became serious with me."

If you'll learn to pray with your whole heart, you will receive an instant manifestation. In Matthew 5:6, Jesus said, "If you hunger and thirst you will be filled." The words "hunger and thirst" also mean to crave or to starve. People do not get into God's dimension, because they are not hungry or thirsty enough for God. They are like spoiled children who eat candy all day long and turn up their noses when a nourishing meal is set before them. They couldn't eat it, anyway, because they are full of junk that is literally killing them.

People, today, have their lives so full of the junk of this temporal world, that they do not have any room for the things of God. They may even become hateful when you talk about the things of God. If we, as Christians, will begin starving out some of the things of this world, the eternal, supernatural, life-changing Word of God will become exciting to read and meditate upon. We will be filled with the supernatural things of God.

When we allow other things in our life to become more important than the things God, it becomes difficult and often impossible to pray with our whole hearts.

In Mark 4:19 Jesus said, "And the cares of this world, deceitfulness of riches, and lust of other things entering in, choke the Word, and it becometh unfruitful."

# IT DOESN'T TAKE LONG

*And in every work that he began in the service of the house of God, and in the law, and in the commandments, to seek his God, he did it with all his heart, and prospered.*

*2 Chronicles 31:21*

Hezekiah knew the secret of seeking the Lord with all of his heart. Hezekiah knew how to pray with his whole heart. God spoke to Isaiah, a prophet of God, and told him that Hezekiah needed to get his house in order, because he was going to die. When God says something, heaven and earth will pass away before it doesn't come to pass. The Scriptures say that Hezekiah set his face to the wall and turned his attention away from everything else. He forgot about any problems, ambitions or concerns, and sought God with his undivided attention. It is evident that Hezekiah prayed with his whole heart. It didn't take long to receive his answer from God.

2 Kings 20:1-6 tells about the same story, adding more details that are not given in the book of Isaiah. Before Isaiah was out of the middle court of Hezekiah's quarters, God spoke to him, and told him to turn back and tell Hezekiah that his prayers had been heard, his tears had been seen, healing would be manifested and 15 years would be added to his life.

In studying this story, I found that Hezekiah's exterior outer court was 600 feet in length. It would only have taken 15 minutes, at most, for Isaiah to leave Hezekiah's presence and walk to the middle court. I have two observations regarding this. First, God is no respecter of persons; what He does for one person, He will do for any. So, we can pray with our whole heart, and God will hear and answer us in no more time than it took for Hezekiah's prayer to be answered. Second, Hezekiah was of the Old Testament. If God will not do for us on a better scale than what He did for all of those in the Old Testament, then Jesus didn't need to come; He would have lived and died in vain. Matthew 11:11 says that you who are least in this era of time are greater than the greatest of the Old Testament.

Jeremiah 33:3 also addresses the concept of praying with our whole heart. God says, "Call (fall down, cry out with your whole heart) to Me, and I will answer you and show you great and mighty things which thou knowest not." He will show you things that are just for you and prepared for you, that no one else has ever seen or heard. He will show you things that have never entered into the heart of anyone. Just simply call out to Him, and love and live for Him with your whole heart.

# CHAPTER 2

# WHAT ARE SIGNS AND WONDERS?

Over the years, I have heard many people talk about Signs and Wonders. My opinion on this topic, however, is different than most. I have written a book entitled, *Neglecting Signs and Wonders is Neglecting the Rapture,* in which I go into detail concerning the true Scriptural meaning of Signs and Wonders. I will only briefly touch on this subject in this book.

I use the following meanings when using the words "Signs and Wonders": "Signs" meaning supernatural miracles in the realm of the senses, confirming the atoning work of Christ, "Wonders" meaning supernatural miracles in the imagination realm, confirming the atoning work of Christ. I believe, from a Scriptural standpoint, that Signs and Wonders mean miracles that the natural, intellectual mind cannot deny.

I arrived at this opinion through the Scripture, and as a result of visions that the Lord ordained. Also, I have extensively researched the topic in resource materials, such as *Strong's Exhaustive Concordance of the Bible*, *W.E. Vine's Book on Old and New Testament Words*, *Young's Concordance*, the King James Bible and the Amplified Bible. My studies began in Pusan, Korea, in 1968, as a 17-year-old soldier, and continue to this day.

Exodus 14:13-29 is a perfect example of a situation in which a wondrous manifestation occurs. The Red Sea is about 1,700 feet deep, but the power of God came into operation, causing the walls of water to form a large passageway through the waters. The floor of the sea became dry ground, as the children of Israel walked to deliverance on the other side.

In Matthew 15:30-38, Jesus healed the multitudes.

In Joshua 10, God hearkened to Joshua's command that the sun and the moon stand still, and they instantly obeyed.

Matthew 14:28 finds Jesus and Peter walking on the sea. Peter received his faith from hearing the Word of God. He heard only one word, "Come." You might be thinking that Peter heard Jesus speak many other times, but so did the other disciples who were in that same boat.

It should also be noted that, today, we have a more sure Word, than those who lived in Biblical times. Therefore, we should be doing that much more.

In 2 Peter 1:17-21, Peter tells us that through the inspiration of the Holy Spirit, the Scriptures are a more sure Word than God speaking in an audible voice. Peter was recalling the transfiguration of Jesus on the mount, when His face did shine in the sun and His raiment was as white as the light. A bright cloud overshadowed them, and a voice out of heaven said, "This is my beloved Son in whom I am well pleased hear ye Him." Peter said, "We have a more sure Word, which is the Scriptures." Yes, the Scripture is surer than God speaking to His own Son in an audible voice.

In Acts 8:39-40, Philip was translated at least 20 miles.

In John 11, Jesus raises Lazarus from the dead, after he had been dead for four days. Once again, an undeniable miracle was instantly manifested in such a way that even the atheist would have to admit that there is a God Who supersedes all gods.

In John 14:12, Jesus said, "Verily, verily I say unto you, he that believeth on Me, the works that I do shall he do also; and greater works than these shall he do; because I go unto My Father." Jesus was closing out His dispensation for a greater dispensation of God to come into existence. Being filled with the Holy Spirit is the fullest expression of God in this world. Ephesians 1:22-23 says, "...the church, which is Christ body the fullness of Him, which filleth all and all." I John 4:17 says, "...as He (God) is; so are we in this world."

John 14:13 continues, "Whatsoever you shall ask in Jesus' name, that will He do, that the Father be glorified in the Son." He is telling us that whatever we ask in His name, He will do it!

In the early 1900's, Dr. Nelson was one of the leading Greek scholars in the world. I've heard Brother Kenneth Hagin talk of the many times he sat under Dr. P.C. Nelson's teachings. During one such minister's meeting, I heard Brother Hagin retell Dr. Nelson's explanation of the phrase in verse 13, "I will do it" to be better understood in the English language as, "If you ask anything in my name, and if it doesn't exist, I will make it for you."

Certainly, it is plain from Scripture that the phrase, "anything that one would ask" would include Signs and Wonders.

# IT IS THE GLORY OF GOD MANIFEST IN MORTAL FLESH

In John 17:22, Jesus prayed that we would have the same glory that He had and has. The word "glory" stands for God's very reputation. Signs and Wonders are something that God wants manifested through His Church of simple believers. Mark 16:17 says that Signs would follow the believer. A person becomes a believer immediately upon accepting Jesus Christ as Lord and Savior.

Ephesians 1:17-23 and 3:14-20 outline a prayer that the Holy Spirit gave to the Church. I have heard Brother Kenneth Hagin say that he had been in the ministry for several years, but it wasn't until he started praying this prayer, that he began to understand the deeper things of God. I can say the same thing with much confidence.

Verse 18 of this prayer says, "Pray that the eyes of our understanding be enlightened (deeply understood in our spirits, minds and flesh) that we may know what is the riches of His glory to us as saints of God." "Glory" in this verse means reputation. God's reputation or glory has many meanings, such as holy or pure, but it is also about Signs and Wonders.

Jesus, the perfect will and voice of God in the earth, said in John 17:18, "As thou (God) has sent Me into this world, even so have I also sent them (us) into the world."

John 17 was Jesus' intercessory prayer for the Church, today, and Jesus always had His prayers answered! According to 2 Corinthians 4:1, we have been given this ministry, this treasure in earthen vessels. The treasure is God's glory, His reputation for the believer, today.

2 Corinthians 3:7 talks about the glory that was in Moses' ministry and life, to such a degree that it caused His face to shine. In 2 Corinthians 3:10, God says that Moses didn't have glory compared to what is available for the believer, today. 2 Corinthians 3:17-18 gives directions as to how we can be changed into this same image of God's glory. This is only accomplished by continuing to look into God's Word. His Word and Spirit change us from glory to a more mature glory.

2 Corinthians 4:6-7 says that this ministry is the knowledge of the glory of God, and we have been given this treasure in earthen vessels. These earthen vessels are our mortal bodies, here, on earth, and will not be found in heaven. In 2 Corinthians 4:10-11, the Scriptures say that the treasure in earthen vessels is the life of Jesus being manifest in our bodies or in our mortal flesh. Signs and Wonders are supposed to occur in a human's mortal flesh.

# THE LEAST OF SALVATION

The most prominent word for "save", both in the Old and New Testament, means health, healing, prosperity, to be made whole, soundness, preservation and deliverance. Modern Bibles, such as the King James Version, New International Version, as well as many others, use words such as *healing*, *health*, *prosperity*, and *deliverance* or *to be made whole*, while the original Greek and Hebrew use the same word to mean all of these terms.

For example, in John 3:17, 47, Ephesians 2:8-9 and Romans 10:9, the word "save" or "saved" is used with the Greek word *sozo*. *Sozo* means healing, health, prosperity, deliverance or to be made whole (see Strong's #4982). The text refers to people receiving salvation, the new birth and eternal divine life from God. Mark 6:56 tells that when Jesus entered into the villages or cities, as many as touched Him were made whole. In this verse, once again, the Greek word *sozo* is used.

Luke 6:6-10 says, "And it came to pass also on another Sabbath, that He entered into the synagogue and taught: and there was a man whose right hand was withered (shrunken, deformed). And the scribes and Pharisees watched Him, whether He would heal on the Sabbath day; that they might find an accusation against Him. But He knew their thoughts, and said to the man which had the withered hand, Rise up, and stand forth in the midst. And he arose and stood forth. Then said Jesus unto them, I will ask you one thing; Is it lawful on the Sabbath days to do good, or to do evil? To save life, or to destroy it?"

Again, the word "save" is the Greek word *sozo*. Jesus was referring to the man's hand being recreated, making that which was not there, to be made whole. In the next verse, that is exactly what happened, "And looking round about upon them all, He said unto the man, Stretch forth thy hand. And he did so: and his hand was restored whole as the other" (verse 10).

Healing, saving, delivering, prosperity and being made whole are all interchangeable terms. I encourage you to expect, have confidence in, and start allowing the ministry of Signs and Wonders to operate in your life for God's glory.

If someone knocked on our door and cried, "Please help me. I don't want to go to hell," we would probably pray Romans 10:9-10 with them. This would give them the assurance of going to heaven, according to the highest authority in existence.

If someone came to our door and cried, "I heard you are a child of the living God and can help me. Please, help me. I am missing an eye (or some other body part)," what would happen? Is the temporal miracle or the eternal more difficult? The missing body part being made whole is a temporal miracle, and to be born again is an eternal miracle. They are asking for a part of salvation, the simplest part, as eternal life is the most difficult part.

There are some people who do not get all there is to get when it comes to salvation. I know of some who don't believe in healing, yet they exhibit some of the most genuine attributes of Christ in their life. I know good Christian people who live with sickness all of their lives, die, and go to heaven. They never received all the salvation that was available to them. I know Christians who live in great financial trouble, but still go to heaven when they die. They also received only a part of salvation. Missing body parts being made instantly whole is just another part of salvation. It is the simplest part, and it is just as legitimate as the rest.

The fact is that if there isn't any manifestation of this wholeness in ministry, salvation doesn't exist because they are the exact same word. If God can instantly do the most difficult, He can do the simplest. Keep in mind the simplicity of salvation, as seen in Ephesians 2:8-9 and

Romans 10:8-10. Also keep in mind that Signs and Wonders are the simplest form of salvation.

# JESUS IS THE SAME

Hebrews 13:8 is clear when it says that Jesus is the same yesterday, today and forever. This was as true during the healings in Jesus' time, as it is today. Several times in His earthly ministry, Jesus ministered to great multitudes that easily numbered 12,000. In every case, Jesus healed (or gave all of *sozo* that was needed) them all. The maimed, in these great numbers, instantly received their body parts. See Matthew 4:23, 8:16, 9:35, 12:15, 14:14 and 15:30-31.

# IT IS ABOUT HAVING GOD'S LITERAL FAITH

*And Jesus answering saith unto them, Have faith in God.*
*Mark 11:22*

Jesus tells us to have faith in God. Some Bible versions translate this as having the God-kind-of-faith. In verse 23, Jesus teaches how to have God's kind of faith. If you believe God's Word, then you should follow Jesus' instructions in Mark 11:22. Here, Jesus said that we could have faith in God, and in the following verse He explained how. Jesus mentioned the word "believing" only one time, and He mentioned the word "saying" three times. So, we should **speak** the promises of God, for which we are believing, three times more than we **believe**. This is not legalism; it is using the power of God. If you want more of God's power, use His principles more.

# CHAPTER 3

# SIGNS AND WONDERS WILL BRING THE LAST DAYS

For many years, I was of the opinion that in the last days God would pour out His Spirit, and there would be Signs and Wonders. To a degree, I still believe that this is true. In looking at the Scriptures, I now plainly see that God will pour out His Spirit in the last days, but it will be because we are already involved in a ministry of Signs and Wonders. This chapter will expound upon the clear doctrine that Signs and Wonders are a ministry of the last days, and that the world will know of God's glory. For further information about this topic, I have written a book entitled, *If We Neglect Signs and Wonders, We Neglect the Rapture.*

# THE GLORIOUS CHURCH

The Church has a job to complete before the rapture can take place. This world must know that God is the only true God, and that He is a good God. The world does not know God, and will not know or understand Him unless we bring Him to their level of understanding, just as He did for the people of Egypt when He delivered the children of Israel. The Egyptians did not accept God, but they could not say that God did not make a way of salvation for them that was on their level and was undeniably God.

Isaiah 34 and 35 clearly highlight what will happen during the end-times. Isaiah 35:2 says that Carmel and Sharon will see the glory (the reputation of God in all of His splendor and might) of the Lord and the excellence of God. *Carmel* refers to small nations or places, and *Sharon* refers to prosperous great places. This passage is in agreement with Luke 3:6, where Jesus said that all flesh shall see the salvation (healing and miracles that are undeniable, such as missing body parts being made instantly whole) of God.

Isaiah 35:3-8 continues, "...the weak hands will be strengthened and the feeble knees will be confirmed. The blinded eyes will be opened and the deaf will receive hearing. The lame will leap as a hart and those unable to speak will receive the ability to speak."

Verse 8 brings attention to the fact that the way of true Godly holiness is for those who are wayfaring. In the Hebrew, wayfaring people are those who live, set the course of their life, and exist because of their conversation. Their lifestyle is based upon the words that come from their mouths. They are the redeemed, living a supernatural life.

This passage of Scripture paints a clear picture of a glorious Church in the last days.

Joel 2:28 says, "...God will pour out His Spirit upon all flesh." This is a depiction of the last days being filled with the ministry of Signs and Wonders. There is further correlation between Joel 2:28-32 and Acts 2:17-21. The Scriptures do not say that everyone will be saved, but they do say that all will experience His Spirit being poured out upon their flesh.

I returned from Monterey, Mexico, where I held a Signs and Wonders Crusade, in which there were more miracles than I could remember. However, some of the local pastors kindly let me know that they disagreed with the healing and giving of miracles to those who were not born again and had no relationship with God. I explained that salvation is a manifold blessing.

The word "salvation" means many things in its original language, both in the Old and New Testament. It means to have eternal life imparted to someone accepting Jesus Christ as their Lord, as well as, healing, to be made whole, to have health or to have financial prosperity.

I told them that there are many Christians who have sickness in their bodies and will still go to heaven. It is evident that they do not have all of the salvation God has offered to the human race. In like manner, a sinner could receive healing or a miracle, and yet not have eternal life. I explained that healings, miracles and Signs and Wonders are tools for evangelism. As Howard Carter said many years ago, "These gifts are the dinner bell for the Gospel."

In this particular crusade, I also noticed that many more people were accepting Jesus as their Lord, and I believe it was because the Gospel was demonstrated to them, rather than being presented as just another convincing speech about the right path to follow. Our records showed that everyone who received healing or a miracle, also accepted Jesus as their Lord. I can understand this, because healing and miracles are demonstrations of God's love.

In fact, when you minister in this fashion, the people should know that miracles and Signs and Wonders are only a small portion of God's love. There is much more love from God to be received, when they accept Jesus as their Lord. Most will go on to experience this fuller salvation. Even if they do not, those who are nearby will see and witness this demonstration of a good and loving Father, and will accept Him and tell others. When all flesh experiences God's Holy Spirit upon them, there remains no excuse to not know the goodness and loving-kindness of God.

Joel 2:30 describes the wonders of the last days. The blood refers to the miracles that take place as a result of the atoning blood of Jesus Christ. The fire refers to the lightning, or rays of light, that are a product of God's power or reputation. According to Habakkuk 3:4, they are also the hiding place of God's power. According to 2 Chronicles 5:13-14, the pillars of smoke refer to God's Shekinah glory. Joel 2:3-11 further illustrates the Signs and Wonders of the last days, where nothing shall escape the great move of God.

"Be glad then, ye children of Zion, and rejoice in the Lord your God: for He hath given you the former rain moderately, and He will cause to come down for you the rain, the former rain, and the latter rain in the first month" (Joel 2:23).

All the former and latter rains of the Lord will take place in one month. If this referred to natural rains on the earth, there would be oceans of water covering every square foot of the earth. If it referred to natural water, there would be such a saturation, that no one could escape the waters. Rather, this passage refers to the great movement and manifestation of God.

The *former rains* signify the greatest moves of God from the beginning of time to this present age, and the *latter rains* signify the greatest moves of God from the present time through the future. It becomes clear that the whole earth will know the ministry of Signs and Wonders in the last days. Everyone will be touched by it, and will be very aware of it.

I Peter 1:5 tells of a salvation that is to be revealed or has been reserved for the last days, "Who are kept by the power of God through faith unto salvation ready to be revealed in the last time."

The word "salvation" in this verse has the same meaning as in Hebrews 2:3, in which salvation refers to Signs and Wonders.

Ephesians 5:25-27 teaches that there will be a glorious Church presented to the Lord. The Church will not be presented until the rapture takes place. A glorious Church will be one that has the very reputation of God, and that is the meaning of the word "glory". If the Church that is to be raptured is glorious, there is once again a ministry of Signs and Wonders for the last days.

I John 3:2 says, "…when the Lord shall appear, we shall be like Him." He will not appear until we are like Him, and to be like the Lord is to have His reputation. To have His reputation is to be involved in the ministry of Signs and Wonders.

I John 3:3 says, "And everyone that has this hope in him purify themselves, even as God, Himself, is pure." The Scripture didn't say that we had to believe or have faith to be pure, as God is pure. It simply said that if you had hope, you would be like Jesus, and become pure, as He is pure. Our Heavenly Father is so good to make such a supernatural impossible, unreachable thing, natural and possible.

# THE WORLD WILL KNOW OF GOD'S GLORY

God wants the world to know of His goodness, and the whole world will know, especially in the last times.

Isaiah 52:10 says that all the ends of the earth shall see the salvation of our God. It says, *shall* see, so it hasn't happened, yet. Isaiah 53 talks about the death of Jesus and the price He paid, "So by His knowledge shall many be justified." "Justified" means to be just like Him (see I John 4:17). Luke 3:6 says that all flesh shall see the salvation of God. Once again, salvation has the same meaning as in Hebrews 2:3.

Salvation is the demonstration of God's supernatural Signs and Wonders. One example of this is found in Exodus 14:13, where Moses said, "...see the salvation of God," and then parted the Red Sea. Salvation in this passage clearly demonstrates the miraculous workings of God.

Psalm 50:23 says, "...(the person) that ordereth their conversation aright (speaks only God-ordained words) will see the salvation of God." God made the excellency of His power available to all of humanity.

Isaiah 66:18 talks about a time when all nations and tongues shall see the glory of God. Isaiah 40:5 says, "And the glory of the Lord shall be revealed, and all flesh shall see it together: for the mouth of the Lord hath spoken it." Never has all of humanity experience the glory, the reputation of God all at once. When the Church comes to the maturity of God's glory, His reputation will flood the earth with the supernatural like the earth has never known or seen.

God has always had a principle of drawing near to those who draw near to Him, when He sees people using His Word to fulfill Signs and Wonders. It so touches His heart that He gives a hundredfold blessing of Signs and Wonders upon and through the doer of His Word.

When the rapture takes place, we shall be like Him. He is coming for a glorious Church, and the Church will be at its ultimate maturity when the rapture takes place.

Isaiah 60:1-2 says, "Arise, shine; for thy light is come and the glory of the Lord is risen upon thee. For, behold, the darkness shall cover the earth and gross darkness the people; but the Lord shall arise upon thee and His Glory shall be seen upon thee."

It is God's glory that will be upon the Church. Those who have the Gospel are anointed to do the works of Jesus. Those who do not have the Gospel, do not have the anointing to do the works to Jesus.

The anointing is first for the preaching of the Gospel. It is second for binding up the broken-hearted, who are oppressed of the devil. Third, it gives liberty to those who are in captivity, under the obsession of the devil. Fourth, it opens the prisons of those who are possessed of the devil. (I go into these three steps of satanic warfare in simpler and

34

greater detail in my book entitled, *Understanding Your Worse Enemy*.) Fifth, the anointing will give you the ability to proclaim the acceptable year of the Lord, as quoted by Jesus in Luke 4:18.

Jesus taught about the time of jubilee as something for all who desire to receive it from the time of His days on earth until the rapture. This is a time of freedom from anything that comes against us. These five areas of anointing are all supernatural, and they are the Signs that follow only those who have the Gospel.

Isaiah 61:11 teaches that "this righteousness will spring forth before all nations, and the world will know of the greatness and riches of the goodness of the Lord." This teaching isn't something we should do only if it is convenient, as it is a commandment from God. Psalm 96:3 says, "Declare His glory among the heathen and His wonders among all people." This is really a commandment from God. However, it is something even more precious than that. It is an invitation to live in the same dimension that God, Himself, lives in, as well as, an opportunity to take others with you.

I Chronicles 16:24 gives this same invitation or ordination. Habakkuk 2:14 says, "The earth shall be filled with the knowledge of the glory of the Lord, as the waters cover the sea." For this knowledge to cover the earth makes it plain that all earth will know of God's glory.

Psalm 105 tells of God bringing His people out of Egypt with Signs and Wonders. Verse 37 says, "...and there was not a feeble person among them." In over two million people, there was no type of sickness or disease. Israel coming out of Egypt is a type of the rapture of the Church. The world will know of a supernatural, victorious Church.

A Church of this caliber will make the news. The Church is to be Christ-like.

God is so full of love and compassion. He has and always will come to our level. Jesus came to Thomas' level, so that he would believe. Thomas said, "Unless I see, I will not believe." Jesus said that it is better to believe and not see. However, Jesus did come to Thomas' level, and Thomas believed. In John 4:48, Jesus also said, "Except you see signs and wonders you will not believe." Then He performed a miracle, so that belief would be manifested. Verse 50 said that the man believed the Word of God, but this belief did not occur until after Jesus had ministered Signs and Wonders in his presence. God loves the whole world, and He will come to anyone's level, as long as it does not violate His Word.

Romans 15:18-19 teaches that the Gentiles became obedient to God's Word, because of Signs and Wonders. God will give the whole world one last chance to become obedient to His Word, as people move into the ministry of Signs and Wonders.

# CHAPTER 4

# UNDERSTANDING THE PRECISE WILL OF GOD CONCERNING MIRACLES

It is God's will for Signs and Wonders to be in manifestation, whenever there is a need for them, in order that people's needs and desires are met and the Father be glorified. We can mature to the place that Signs and Wonders come into operation, as we will, for God is always willing.

Hebrews 5:13-14 and I Peter 2:1-2 teaches that the Word of God will mature us. By simply reading God's Word, we can come into an understanding and maturity for Signs and Wonders to start working in our lives, that the Father may be glorified. I Corinthians 12:11 says, "But all these worketh that one and the self-same spirit, dividing to every man severally as he will."

According to English grammar, the word "man" is an antecedent, in which the pronoun "he" refers to mankind and not to the Spirit. The word for which a pronoun stands is called its *antecedent*. Pronouns should have definite antecedents, and should be placed as close to their antecedents as possible. A pronoun should not appear to refer to either of two antecedents.

So, regardless of what tradition has taught, proper English grammar declares that "he" refers to man and not to God in this passage. (When tradition teaches this doctrine, they usually use I Corinthians 12:11, and interpret it as the gifts of the Spirit are divided to every man severally as the *Holy Spirit* wills.)

As I was teaching this material at a Signs and Wonders conference in Monterey, Mexico, one of the Pastors told me that in the Spanish Bible the pronoun "he" refers to *humanity* and not to the Holy Spirit.

Oftentimes, people will use John 3:34 as another supporting verse to show that God that gave the Holy Spirit to Jesus without measure. The insinuation is that humanity is given God's Holy Spirit by measure. The words "unto him" in John 3:34 would solidify this train of thought. The words "unto him" are italicized in most Bibles, indicating that they are not in the original, correct writing. God gives His Holy Spirit without measure, not only to Jesus, but to humanity, as well.

I am not as interested in disproving their doctrine, as I am proving that all of the gifts of the Holy Spirit and the fullness of God are to be in manifestation as man wills. God is always willing to promote His goodness to whatever degree, in order to bless humanity. According to the Scriptures, this is the will of God concerning this issue.

The gifts of the Spirit come into operation as your will comes into agreement with God's will to bless humanity to whatever degree needed. I Corinthians 13:15 says, "I will pray in the Spirit and I will sing in the Spirit." This contains the understood principle that I can pray or sing in the Spirit, as well as I can sing or pray with my understanding. Speaking in tongues is the least of the gifts, but it is the prerequisite for the others.

This gift is in operation as a person wills, and not only as God wills. There is an experience in tongues that deals with diversity of tongues and is instigated by God, however, this gift comes after we have instigated the simple form of tongues. There is a gift of speaking in tongues that is supernatural and comes from God as the person wills, not only as God wills.

In John 14:12-14, Jesus tells that the works that He did, shall we do, also. Twice, Jesus said that if we will ask anything in His name, He would do it. In order to be able to do everything that Jesus did, and have the privilege to ask for whatever we want to be done an have it done, we will have to be able to minister all the gifts and the anointing of God, as this is what Jesus did.

# GOD'S WORD IS HIS WILL

The Word of God is the will of God. Ephesians 1:9 says, "Having made known unto us the mystery of His (God's) will..." This is a truth that is in the past tense. Ephesians 3:3 says, "How that by revelation He (God) make known unto me (Paul) the mystery." The will of God is referred to as "the mystery". The book of Ephesians is all one letter.

"Epistle" means letter. Ephesians 3:4 says, "Whereby, when you read, you may understand my knowledge in (or of) the mystery of Christ." When you read the Word of God, you read the will of God.

In Ephesians 5:17, God gives us a commandment to be not unwise, but understanding of the Lord's will. If God commands us to do something we cannot do, He would be bad and unfair. God commands us to know His will, because we can know it by simply reading His Word. God's commandments are privileges of opportunity, and not a type of religious bondage.

I Thessalonians 4:2-3 says, "For you know what commandments we gave you by the Lord Jesus, for this is the will of God." The commandments or words of God are God's will.

According to Deuteronomy 29:29, the secret things belong to God, but the things that are revealed (published, shown openly) [2] belong unto us and to our children forever, that we may do all the words of the law (the words or commandments of God).

Most of the time, the scholars who translated our modern Bible did a superior job. However, any time words are translated from one language to another, problems can arise. In this case, the word "revealed" in Deuteronomy 29:29, lets us know the written Word belongs to us that we may do it. If we do not do it, we will not enjoy the fullness of what God has for us. I Corinthians 2:9 teaches, "God has things prepared for them that love Him that eye hath not seen, ear has not heard, but God hath revealed them unto us by His Sprit, yes, even the deep things of God." This revealing comes through the Spirit and John 1:1 says, "In

---

[2] Strong, James. *Strong's Exhaustive Concordance.* Massachusetts: Hendrickson Publishers, pg. 843.

the beginning the Word was with God and was God." These are Scriptures that validate the concept that the Spirit and the Word of God are the same.

There is a hidden will in man that only man's spirit would know. In like manner, God's Spirit knows more about God than anyone else. Through the Spirit of God or the Word of God, we can know things that are of that realm.

I Corinthians 2:13 goes into greater detail about how the Holy Spirit does this by comparing Scripture with Scripture.

# LOOKING AT GOD'S WILL

There are many verses that tell us what we have and can do with God's will. Brother John Osteen often said that he could do what God said he could do, and that he was who God said he was. That is a good Scriptural statement to keep in mind during this segment.

2 Peter 1:3-4 says, "According as God's divine power (the greatest power in existence) hath (past tense) given us all things that pertain to this life and God likeness (which is the true meaning of Godliness), through (or by) the knowledge of God (there is only one way to get the knowledge of God, and that is by the Holy Scriptures) that hath called us to glory and virtue.

We have been called unto glory (God's reputation) and virtue (God's power), according to the knowledge of God's Word.

Verse 4 calls attention to the exceeding great and precious promises of God's Word. It is through these promises that

41

we become partakers of God's divine nature. If you are a partaker of God's nature, and have already been given everything that pertains to God's likeness, you could move into any of the gifts of God at your discretion.

When you begin to see these truths, and allow God's will to become your will, supernatural life starts becoming active, when the need is present. In John 17:18, Jesus said, "As He was sent from the Father in like manner now are we sent by Him." Everything that Jesus did is available to us, today.

In John 17:22, Jesus prayed to the Father, and asked Him to give all of humanity the same glory that He had. Jesus always prayed the perfect will of God, and His prayers were always answered. So, this is now ours. However, just because something exists does not necessarily mean that you know it or that you know how to use it.

If someone gave you a rocket ship, and you did not know how to use it, it would not mean that it was not yours.

Hosea 4:6 teaches us that God's people are destroyed for a lack of knowledge. Signs and Wonders have not been in manifestation among God's people, because they either do not know what belongs to them, or they do not have knowledge to operate with the gifts.

In John 3:34, the Scriptures tell us that God gives His Spirit without measure. If God gives us His Spirit without measure, at our will we can do all the mind and intent of God. In case you believe this verse refers only to Jesus, there are other verses that support this teaching. In Matthew 28:18, Jesus said that all miracle-working power was given to Him. In Ephesians 1:22-23, Jesus gave all things to the Church, which is His body, the fullness of Him that filleth all and all. If the will of God is to be accomplished in this world, we, the body of Christ, who is the highest expression of God in this world, are going to have to do it.

Colossians 1:26 talks about the mystery of the ages, which is now made manifest in us. It is Christ in us, the hope of God being glorified. There was a time when God had so much hope that He would be well glorified, that He sent Jesus to this earth. Jesus did His job, perfectly. Now, God has that same hope in us. God had confidence that Jesus would adequately pay the price, so that we would be able to replace Him in this earth. The Church is the living Christ reincarnated.

John 16:24 says, "Ask and you shall receive that your joy be full." The decision is yours. In John 6:28-29, the disciples asked Jesus what they should do that they might work the works of God; what prerequisite would they have to meet in order to function in the miracle-working power of God? Jesus gave us the answer: Believe on Him that God hath sent. Keep in mind that Jesus was, is and always will be the Word of God (see Revelation 19:13, Hebrews 13:8 and John 1:14).

If you want the miracle-working power of God to be in operation, find Scripture to support doing it and do it. If you only read it and do not do it, you do not Scripturally believe that it is true. Genesis 11 tells a story about an ungodly group of people who were building a tower, in order to gain the power of God. In verses 6 and 7, God said that if He did not stop them, nothing that they could imagine would be restrained from them. That is what God, Himself, said about them.

Now, these people were ungodly people. These people were of the Old Testament. If Godly people cannot supersede ungodly people, then we are serving the wrong god. We are of the New Testament, and it is established upon better promises than the Old Testament. It is not better, if we do not have more than the Old Testament saints or the heathen. If we as children of God cannot have the blessings of the Old Testament, then Jesus died in vain, and He did not die in vain (see Hebrews 7:19-22, 8:6, 10:1).

# CHAPTER 5

# GOD'S GRACE: THE PREREQUISITE FOR SIGNS AND WONDERS

Scripture teaches that God is greater than satan. Love is greater than hate. Righteousness is greater than unrighteousness. Grace is greater than sin. God and His works are greater than satan and all of his works. This chapter establishes the fact that God's grace is greater than sin. Scripture makes it evident that God's power and anointing can only be in operation, based upon unmerited favor. When you understand the holiness and perfection of God, you come to the perfect understanding that the only way any person could ever receive anything from God, would have to be on the basis of God's goodness and His unmerited favor.

Ephesians 2:8-9 says, "For by grace you are saved through faith." We are saved by grace (totally unmerited favor) through faith. Faith is believing what God's Word says, and then acting like it is true with every part of our being. So then, we are saved by God's grace, through or by believing what God's Word says, and then acting like it is true.

The Book of Judges tells the story of Samson's life. Samson had a big problem avoiding illicit sexual behavior with several different women. Judges 16:1 says that Samson went to Gaza and saw a harlot (a prostitute), and he went in unto her. In verse 2, the Gazites found out where Samson was and lay in wait for him all night. The soldiers were waiting in the gate of the city and were quiet all the night saying, "In the morning, when it is day, we shall kill Samson." In verse 3, Samson laid with a prostitute until midnight. He then rose and took the doors and the two posts of the gate and went away with them, carrying them upon his shoulders to the top of a hill that is before Hebron.

There is a great magnitude to this miracle. According to Judges 15:15, Samson had the reputation of single-handedly slaying a thousand men. The men waiting for him were most likely a larger group of men than this, or they wouldn't have thought that they could overcome him. The previous battle, described in Judges 14, had to have been still fresh in their minds.

Again, proving the magnitude of this miracle was that Samson carried the doors and two gateposts from Gaza to the top of the hill that is before Hebron (Hebron is located 190 miles from Gaza). This was a supernatural event, a clear manifestation of God's miracle-working power in operation. Samson illustrated a major point. If God will allow His miracle-working power to operate for a man deep in sin, then His anointing will be in operation for us to use to honor and glorify His name through miracles. It was very foolish for Samson to pull up the gates of the city and carry them 190 miles. There are many greater miracles that would bless humanity, such as, commanding legs that have been removed to manifest, so that people would experience blessings, both naturally and spiritually, that God be exalted.

Another observation is that Samson called on God's miracle-working power, as he crawled out of bed with a prostitute, yet God heard and answered Samson's request. This did not happen based on Samson's close walk with God, but rather through the grace of God. You can live in sin, and God's goodness and grace will work for you, because God's grace is greater than sin. However, there is also another law in operation, and that is the law of sin and death.

Romans 8:1-2 tells about the two laws that are in existence. The first is the law of the Spirit of life that comes from God. The second is the law of sin and death that comes from satan. The law of the Spirit of life cannot be stopped from operation, as God causes this law to operate. Nothing, not even sin or satan, can stop this law.

God is not unrighteous or dishonest. He does not interfere if a person willingly chooses to live by the law of sin and death. In Judges 16:27-31, Samson's eyes were put out, because he knew and was willing to operate in the law of sin and death. He put his hands upon two pillars that supported a large building. The roof of the building had 3,000 people on it (the pillars must have been quite large in order to support that many people). Keep in mind that God knows everything; He knows every thought in our minds. Samson said, "Lord, let me avenge myself to destroy all of these people (and myself as well)." Samson asked God to give even greater anointing on his life, so that he could die, and God did it.

God's grace is greater than sin. Samson knew about the grace of God, and it worked for him, even while he was deep in sin. God is no respecter of persons; it will work for you the same way. God is the same yesterday, today and forever. Keep in mind, that if you want to operate in both laws, like Samson, who was tortured by having his eyes burned out with a hot iron, the decision is yours.

Call on the power of God and know that it is only by His grace that miracles, as the world has never seen before, will come to be manifested. Discover the riches of His goodness toward you, and you will not want to sin. God is greater than satan and all of satan's laws. The pleasures of sin are putrefying in comparison to the pleasures that God offers humanity. According to John 14:27, God has a peace (a tranquil lifestyle) that passes all knowledge. Call on the power of God, and know that it is only by His grace that miracles will be manifested. Discover the riches of His goodness toward you.

# JESUS HEALS THEM ALL

I want us to do a small study of the miracle ministry of Jesus, looking only at the book of Matthew. In Matthew 4:23-24, Jesus went about all of Galilee teaching in their synagogues and preaching the Gospel of the kingdom and healing all.

In Matthew 8:16, in the region of Capernaum, Jesus healed all who were sick.

Matthew 9:35 says, "Jesus went about all the cities and He healed every sickness and every disease." Many did not intend to become followers of Christ, even if He healed them, yet He healed them all.

In Matthew 12:15, "Great multitudes followed Him and He healed them all."

In Matthew 14:14, "Great multitudes followed Him and He healed them all."

In Matthew 15:30, "Great multitudes followed Him and He healed them all." If you would take a great multitude out of any city in the world, today, there would be every kind of sinful person that you could imagine in need of healing or wholeness. It was a great manifestation of God's grace that was being depended upon, and Jesus is the same yesterday, today and forever.

The Book of Matthew clearly demonstrates that God's miracle-working power has one major prerequisite, and that is grace. Jesus went about all of Galilee, healing all. There must have been a considerable number of people in all of Galilee, of every sinful nature you can think of, who needed healing. Jesus healed them all, saint and sinner, alike.

In I Corinthians 1:7, Paul said that the Church at Corinth had all of the gifts of the Spirit of God in operation. All of the gifts of the Spirit can be criticized by skeptics as being a manipulation of man, with the exception of the gift of working miracles. There can be no trickery or deception when a person born without legs instantly has them manifested, or when a person of God stands before a nation and commands a sea (1,700 feet in depth) to part, and it does. Modern science at its best cannot deny that a God of such feats would have to be a God of no competition. The Church of Corinth had all of the gifts of the Spirit in full operation.

In I Corinthians 3:1-3, Paul rebuked the Church and called them babes or immature Christians, as well as, carnal Christians. It is only by the grace of God for immature, carnal Christians to have all of the gifts of the Spirit operating in their lives. Galatians 5:4 says, "Christ is become of no effect unto you, whosoever of you are justified (receives anything from God) by the law (efforts of humanity) you are fallen from grace. If Christ is become of no effect to us, and we have fallen from grace, we are eternally hell bound. Only by grace and through faith in Jesus Christ can anyone receive eternal life.

You must rely totally upon God's grace for the greatest miracle (eternal life) and understand that all salvation (including healing and the manifestation of miracles) comes in the same way. If you try another way, you will not only not see results, but you also will fall from grace, and Christ will be of no effect in you.

I Corinthians 3:13 tells us that we have been called unto liberty, but warns us to not use liberty for an occasion to the flesh. He has given us such liberty or grace, that we can sin, and His grace is sufficient. But don't do it. God's grace is a license to sin, but only a fool would use a liberty that is so full, so supernatural, for the lowest form of pleasure – sin.

Once we understand how awesome, pure and holy God and everything He has is, we can understand that the only way to receive or be in God's presence is on the basis of His divine grace. We can become like God through His grace, and understand that the smaller issues of His power exists by that same grace (see I Peter 1:15-16).

In Matthew 10:8, Jesus gave His disciples the command to heal the sick, cleanse the lepers, raise the dead, cast out devils, freely (gratuitously) you have received, so freely (gratuitously) give. The only way to receive such divine, supernatural power is by grace. Once you understand how freely and easily it is received, you will understand how freely and easily it can be given away.

This power belongs to us, just as it did to the disciples to Jesus' day. Jesus said in John 17:18, "As thou (God) hast sent me into the world, even so have I also sent them (us) into the world." All of chapter 17 should be read in order to understand that it was the intercessory prayer of Jesus for all people; from the moment He prayed this prayer until the end of time. Jesus prayed that we, today, would have the same glory that He had in John 17:22.

Hebrews 10:1 tells that the law, the Old Testament, could not make people perfect (complete in growth, be of full age to be fully matured). Verse 14 tells that it is only through one offering, the Lord Jesus, that God made a way whereby people can be made perfect.

A major calling on my life is to teach people how they can mature spiritually and be perfect, unto the fullness of Christ, so that they will do the same things that Jesus did during His time on earth (see Ephesians 4:11-13). There is only one way that I can teach people this, and that is through the ordained testament of grace, the New Testament.

We are of the dispensation of grace, and whatever God did for any one person in the Old Testament, He will do for us of the New Testament. According to Romans 4:2-6, if Abraham was justified (righteous, Holy, to be like God) by works (anything he could do to earn something from God), then he could glory (boast). Abraham believed God, and this was the grounds that it was counted unto him for righteousness (to be like God). Those that worketh (earn by their deeds) to receive righteousness (if it would be possible, but it isn't), their righteousness would be by debt and not by grace. But to those that worketh not (they love God, and have love deeds) their deeds are not a meriting system to earn something from God, but instead they simply believe on Jesus and all His words of grace, that justifieth the ungodly, their faith is counted for righteousness. God imputeth (causes it to be a reality) righteousness without the deeds (legalism) of the law."

If you think that the things you have, and the holiness you live are based upon your own actions, you have a counterfeit, and have been cheated and deceived. Romans 3:28 says that a person is justified (made just like God) by faith without the deeds of the law. Anything and everything we receive from God is based upon what He has done, and not upon what we have done or could ever do.

# CHAPTER 6

# GREATER RESULTS WHEN ONE IS SPIRIT-FILLED

This chapter will show that a person can have greater results ministering Signs and Wonders, if they are Spirit-filled. A person can minister miracles and healings without being Spirit-filled and have results, but greater results come if one is Spirit-filled. A Spirit-filled person is one who speaks with tongues on a daily basis and walks in God's love. According to Galatians 5:22-23, the fruits of the Holy Spirit (character) are established in that person's life because of God's unconditional love.

The Spirit-filled person exhibits joy when circumstances say that they shouldn't have joy. They walk in peace in the midst of storms. They are long-suffering when wrongs have been committed towards them over and over again. They are patient and kind to their offenders. The Spirit-filled-person is gentle, when harshness is deliberated towards them. They exhibit goodness, when dishonesty would give them an advantage, and faithfulness, when it seems there isn't a reward in the world for it. They are meek, when they have been rudely imposed upon, and exhibit temperance just like Jesus, Who is the same yesterday, today and forever.

# THE GIFTS OF THE SPIRIT

I Corinthians 12:4 says that there are many different gifts, but they all come through the same Holy Spirit. Therefore, all gifts belong to Him. If the Holy Spirit abides in me, I have all of His gifts abiding in me. The closer relationship I have with the Holy Spirit, the closer experience I will have with the gifts of the Spirit.

I Corinthians 14:14-15 (Amplified Version) teaches that when we pray in tongues, we pray by the Holy Spirit with our spirit. In Ezekiel 36:26-27, a prophesy is given in detail concerning this same truth. "A new heart (soul or mind) also will I (God) give you, and a new spirit (a God-like spirit) will I put within you, and I will take away the stony heart (the dead spirit that must be born again)...And I will put My Spirit within you, then you will be able to walk in God's statues, and you will be able to keep and do all of God's Words."

This passage is about the New Testament dispensation, in which a person can be born again with a Christ-like spirit and have the ability to have a new mind, that is the mind of Christ. Philippians 2:5 says, "Let this mind be in you which was in Christ." After this, you will have the ability to have the very Spirit of God abide in your spirit. One must be born again before the Holy Spirit can abide in their spirit, and that is a different experience than that of the new birth.

Ezekiel 36 shows that the Holy Spirit can and should abide in our spirits after we are born again. This is also confirmed in John 7:37-39. As God's Spirit abides in our spirit, we will see the gifts of the Holy Spirit in our lives, because wherever the Spirit of God goes, His gifts follow.

# THE HOLY SPIRIT TEACHES
# THE DEEP THINGS OF GOD

In John 16:12-15, Jesus said, "I have many things to say unto you, but you cannot bear them now. Howbeit when He, the Spirit of truth, is come, He will guide you into all truth." Jesus was saying that He had and has many things to say to us and to teach us. He has information that will progress us I every area of our lives.

This information cannot be transmitted by articulate or audible speech. This information cannot even be understood with the natural mind. The Holy Spirit teaches this information to those whose spirits have been born again, and who have become partakers of God's divine nature.

This information is spiritual and divine. Verse 14 says that it will glorify Christ, and will be nothing more than the pure Word of God. However, it can only be taught and understood spiritually, or it becomes the letter of the law. Many have tried to teach the Word of God without the Holy Spirit's influence, and that always brings death.

Simply teaching the Word does not give grace, joy, happiness or life to its hearers. It is nothing more than teaching, that is uninspired by God. Ephesians 4:29-30 identifies this as corrupt communication that grieves, stops or hinders the Holy Spirit. It is evil speaking. We must have an experience with the Holy Spirit, if we want to know the things that the natural world and our minds cannot teach us. It is the Holy Spirit that will take us to the greater, deeper things of God, that we may become an instrument of God's anointing. The greater the experience you have with the Holy Spirit, the more effective you will be.

I Corinthians 2:9-14 says, "As it is written, eye hath not seen, nor ear heard, neither have entered into the heart of mankind, the things which God hath prepared for them that love Him."

There are some things that God has for us, individually, that are beyond the human capacity to understand; God has revealed them unto us by His Spirit. Can you see that the Holy Spirit will reveal things to us, that man with all of his sensibilities cannot even understand? For the Holy Spirit searches all things, yes, even the deep things of God.

"...and if we receive the Spirit of God we then will know the things that God has already freely given us. Which things also we speak, not in the words which man's wisdom teacheth, but which the Holy Ghost teacheth; comparing spiritual things with spiritual" (verses 12-13).

The Holy Spirit will tell you something, and then give you many confirmations that prove it, by comparing spiritual with spiritual.

Verse 14 continues, "The natural man receiveth not the things of the Spirit of God: for they are foolishness unto him: neither can he know them, because they are spiritually discerned (understood and received)."

Many times I have had the experience of trying to teach someone something that I clearly understand, while giving many Scriptures to support what I'm teaching, but the other person is unable to relate to or understand what I was trying to teach. It is difficult to teach Scripture to someone who is not born again. If a person is not born again, they can understand very little of the Holy Scriptures. Everyone has been given a measure of faith to help them know that there is a Superior Being, Who wants to be their Savior, but you need to be born again to progress in God.

A second great hindrance is found in attempting to teach Scripture to someone who is not yet filled with the Holy Spirit, in accordance with what has been mentioned in this book. One example of this is people who do not believe in speaking in tongues and walking in the Spirit; neither do they believe in miracles or healings. They feel that these things have passed away.

There is a great difference of belief between people who speak in tongues and those who do not. The first group has a closer relationship with the Lord than does the second group. Therefore, they have a deeper insight or understanding of the mind, intent and will of the Lord. I believe we ought to be filled with the Holy Spirit in the same way the Apostles were, because we are both of the same dispensation. We can do what they did and have right-standing with God they way they did.

# HOW THEY HOLY SPIRIT PROGRESSES US

In John 16:12-15, Jesus said that the Holy Spirit would guide us after He was gone from the earth. Jesus left a Scriptural pattern, which is the dispensation we will be in until the rapture of the Church. 2 Corinthians 5:1-4 gives an explanation of an experience that was not possible in the Old Testament. In the last 100 years, the full-gospel people have referred to this experienced as "praying through". It is an experience that is, now, almost obsolete among Charismatic and Pentecostal people. I only mention this group of people, because no other group would consider such an experience. Even the groups that have considered it, have come to the place that they, as a whole, know very little or almost nothing about the experience. I cannot do justice concerning this subject in this small portion of the book, as this subject is a book within itself. However, I do want to make this statement about praying through. 2 Corinthians 5:1-4 is a good Scriptural description of the experience of praying through. You can pray with such determination and hunger for the deeper things of God, until you are unaware of this natural world. In doing this, you will experience the great richness of God's goodness, and you will be in the complete fullness of the presence of the Holy Spirit's realm.

I have listened to and read about many people who have had near-death experiences. They entered the presence of the Lord and came back. They all come back changed. Often they change from being bad people to being good, Godly people filled with loving-kindness and mercy. This experience is similar to that of "praying through" as described in 2 Corinthians 5. In fact, it could be the same experience reached in a different way. A person praying in tongues with their whole heart, until they have "prayed through" the flesh in to the realm of the Spirit, initiates this experience.

Some have reached this place through a near-death experience, in which the flesh was cancelled out to the degree that they were only aware of the realm of the Spirit. Some people actually die and have this experience, and supernaturally return to tell about it.

2 Corinthians 5:1-2 says, "We know that if our earthly house (our natural, physical bodies) were dissolved, we have a building of God, a house not made with hands, eternal in the heavens." You must have an eternal building of God, before you can have this experience. You must be born again and a partaker of God's divine nature before you can have this experience. Verse 2 says, "For we groan earnestly desiring to be clothed upon with our house which is from heaven."

After a person is born again, there must be this groaning. In the Greek, the word "groan" is defined as praying inaudibly and earnestly to be clothed. In other words, to be totally covered, enveloped by the house that is not natural, but is only supernatural and spiritual from God.

Also, after a person is born again, they must realize that the new birth is only the beginning of a supernatural, spiritual life. God has more for us than we can think or imagine, if we just read the Scriptures and believe the simplicity and earnestness found in them.

2 Corinthians 5:3 tells us that once we learn to be clothed by this experience, we will find that life without it is void and empty, like being naked. If that is so, we shall not be found naked, if we are clothed. If we live in and with this

experience, we will not be found naked. Our lives will have heavenly purpose.

2 Corinthians 5:4 says, "For we that are in this tabernacle do groan, being burdened: not for that we would be unclothed, but clothed upon, that mortality might be swallowed up of life." We, who earnestly desire this deeper experience, know that it is an experience in which mortality is swallowed up by a great life. In the Greek, the word "zoe" is used in this passage for the word "life". It means life in its most absolute. This is life the way God, Himself, has it.

Romans 8:22-26 also gives a description of the Holy Spirit progressing beyond what can be experienced in the natural. It is a description of praying beyond the natural into the supernatural with the help of the Holy Spirit. Verses 22-23 say, "...the whole of creation groans and travails (expecting relief form suffering)...We groan within ourselves."

Our spirits continuously long, desire and need deeper experiences form the real of the Spirit of God. As in the natural, we need food or we will die. Also, in the natural, we cannot live on baby food, or we will become weak and die, prematurely. In the natural, a healthy person cannot live on the same kind of food year after year, because they wouldn't receive the proper nutrition, and would become very discontent. Just as this is true for our physical bodies, it is also that God has made this true in our spiritual lives. We must progress spiritually or we will die. Our spirit groans to have a supernaturally continuous progression from the natural into the spiritual, as well as, from an unsatisfying lifestyle to one that is supernaturally satisfying. This is a lifestyle the way our Father has it.

Romans 8:24-25 tells us that this is a deeper salvation than that which can be related to with the senses or in the natural realm. This hope of salvation is not seen with the natural eye, because it is not of the natural. Only the Holy Spirit can progress you to this place of fuller salvation.

Romans 8:26-27 teaches the details of how this experience comes into manifestation. Verse 26 says, "Likewise, the (Holy) Spirit also helpeth our infirmities (weaknesses): for we know not what we should pray for as we ought: but the (Holy) Spirit maketh intercession (intercepts pains, sorrows, problems) for us with groanings which cannot be uttered (with articulator or natural speech)."

Since we do not have the capability to know how to speak or pray to a Creator, Who is more holy, pure and perfect than we could ever imagine with our natural minds, the Holy Spirit provides a way. That way is when He prays through us in a heavenly language, speaking in a deeper tongue, that is not the initial tongue you receive when you first receive the Holy Spirit into your Spirit.

The most intelligent person who has ever lived couldn't begin to know how to pray to such a Creator. This speaking or praying is done in the fashion of groanings or sighs from deep down within one's spirit. Many times you will hear these sounds from people at a funeral, because of a deep loss. We have a deeper loss if we are not clothed with the life God has for us. When a person has been filled with the Holy Spirit, they will often articulate these groans or sighs with tongues, which are a deeper speech, initiated by the Holy Spirit.

Not only do we not know how to pray to such a Supreme Creator, but do not know what to pray for. Our Heavenly Father has blessings beyond our understanding.

Ephesians 3:19 says that God has a love for us that passes all knowledge. If God has things to bless us beyond our ability to understand, then we need some supernatural help to know what to pray or ask for. The Holy Spirit does this for us when we submit to this type of deeper experience, that only the He can take (progress) us into.

Romans 8:27 teaches us that no one could know the mind of another anymore than one's own spirit. In like manner, no one knows the mind of God better than His own Holy Spirit, and it is through God's Spirit that this type of praying is done. God prays His perfect will through us.

If you submit to Romans 8:22-27, then verse 28 belongs to you, as well. All things work together for our good when we love God (also, yield to His calling in your life), if we have gone into this deeper progression by the Holy Spirit.

I Samuel 10:6 talks about this deeper experience. If you experience this deeper progression, you will be changed into another person, and begin to have knowledge and power to do whatever needs to be done. You will know that God is with you. If you see a need that calls for supernatural Signs and Wonders to be manifested, you will know you can yield to that call. Samuel was of the Old Testament, and whoever is least in the New Testament is greater than the greatest of the Old Testament. So, if this experience happened to Saul, who wasn't near the greatest of the Old Testament, then how much more for us of the New Testament. Even Jesus said that the Holy Spirit would progress us beyond what even He (Jesus) could do in the flesh.

## CHAPTER 7

# LEARNING HOW TO RELEASE GOD'S ANOINTING

In this chapter, I will share what Jesus said to me in the vision I had on September 28, 1984. I will also break down into simple details, how to release God's anointing into people's lives, so that their needs may be met (even to the degree of people who are missing body parts, being made instantly whole).

When you have a vision, an appearance of a spirit, there are volumes of information that are transmitted in the realm of the spirit. As you meditate on the experience, the information is transmitted into the realm of the soul or intellect. The more you meditate and think about what has been transmitted into the realm of the intellect, the more it becomes manifested in your very natural presence.

# THE SIMPLE TRUTH OF RELEASING GOD'S ANOINTING

After Jesus told me to pray with my whole heart, I studied the Bible from Genesis to Revelations to find Scripture to support what He had said, as well as, to give me greater understanding of what it means to pray with your whole heart. The more I studied the doctrine, the further I seemed to get away from the truth.

We can turn the Spirit into law, and it makes the life and grace of God's Word ineffective. I believe that is what I was doing. I was so over-zealous, that instead of simply doing what Jesus had told me to do, I was looking for something more complicated. Since then, I have learned that there are two major factors in understanding the Holy Scriptures and the realm of God. First, if it isn't **good**, God isn't in it. Second, if it isn't **simple**, God isn't in it. Often times, we preachers make things so difficult, that it takes the simplicity of a grade school student to get us back on track.

After several months of getting further away from the reality of what Jesus had told me, I grew somewhat discouraged, and decided to forget the subject for a while. A short time after that decision, the Holy Spirit told me to turn to Matthew 6:22. Using that verse, the Holy Spirit explained to me what Jesus meant when He said for me to pray with my whole heart.

Since that moment, when I lay hands on people, I can and do release God's anointing, and about 90 percent of the time, I see instant manifestations. Up until that time, I did not see as many results. I believe that the more I grow, the more proficient I will become.

This teaching or revelation that the Lord gave me is simply the Divine Scriptures, that are equally available to all of us. It will work for anyone, as God is no respecter of persons. This chapter is designed to simplify this doctrine, so that the whole Body of Christ can do the work of the ministry of Christ, as spelled out in Ephesians 4:11-13.

# SINGLE-MINDED

Matthew 6:22 says, "The light of the body is the eye: if therefore thine eye be single, thy whole body shall be full of light." I will explain this passage in the way the Holy Spirit simplified it for me. The light is God's glory, power and anointing for the body, which includes the spirit, mind and physical body. God's glory comes through the eye (one's spiritual and mental eye).

Both the spiritual eye and the mental eye can work so closely together that they become one. The mental eye must make the first step of yielding to God's anointing. God's anointing (His power) comes into manifestation beginning with the mental eye. If your mental eye will be single-focused upon only receiving God's anointing for whatever it is that you're needing or desiring, then your whole person, spirit, mind and flesh shall be full of God's light, which is His anointing or power.

With God it is just as simple for His anointing to cause a missing arm to be manifested, as it is to remove a headache. Not all humans have a tendency to think that way.

Let me give you an example of how simple it is for a beginner to start releasing God's anointing. Let's say a person has a headache. Ask them about the pain, in as much detail as you can think of. If they haven't been to the doctor, which is usually the case with a headache, ask them to describe the pain. You need to be specific, so that you can be more single-minded.

Ask them to close their eyes, so they can be more single-minded, as well. (When our eyes are open, it is easier to be double-minded.) Lay your hand on the area where the pain is located. There may be times you may not want to lay your hand on them, because the physical contact alone may hinder them being able to remain single-minded. This is perfectly Scriptural, as the power of God is in His Word. We can just speak to the situation in accordance with God's Word and be very successful.

Ask them to not speak or think about anything else. Light and darkness cannot occupy the same space. Tell them to force their minds to focus only upon receiving. Command the pain that they described to leave. You will notice that Jesus always eliminated what He didn't want before He built what He did want. Luke 13:11-13 illustrated this point. Jesus first dealt with the spirit of infirmity before He laid His hands on the lady for healing. You must eliminate the root of the problem before you can minister the cure or regeneration. It's as if someone has given you a piece of land to build your dream home, but a shack sits in the exact location of where you wish to build. You must first eliminate the shack, before you can build the new home. I believe where a problem exists, a demon is involved. So, get rid of the demon first, and then cure what he has harmed.

Command that portion of their body to relax. As one relaxes, they are yielding. In this case, they are yielding to the anointing that is always available. As you speak, see a stream of light (which is God's anointing) leaving your hand and going into the portion of their body that needs healing.

Be careful, because it can be very easy for you to become double-minded while ministering the anointing. The demons of hell will be there to intimidate you, and try to get you to be double-minded. "A double-minded person will not receive anything from the Lord" (James 1:7-8).

You must refuse any kind of distracting thought while ministering the anointing, while teaching them to do the same. Insignificant thoughts will come, such as, "Are you sure you're praying or ministering, correctly?" or "What are you going to do or look like if this person isn't healed?"

The not-so-obvious, yet real and powerful demons are there to hinder you. Understand that they are there to keep you and the person for whom you are ministering, from being single-minded. If they can defeat you in this smallest area, you will never progress to a natural manifestation. There are different operations of the Spirit of God and different ways to minister to people, but while ministering in this way, make sure the person remains quiet. You cannot talk and hear at the same time. Make sure that no one else is talking or touching them, either, hindering them from being single-minded.

# YOUR MIND IS THE DOORWAY TO YOUR SPIRIT

There are ways that the fullness of God's power, His anointing, is made real to us, based upon how we allow God's Word into our minds, and how we keep it there. Our minds determine what kind of a spirit we will have, and our spirits determine what kind of a life we will have in the natural.

Romans 8:6 says, "For to be carnally-minded is death; but to be spiritually-minded is life and peace." In John 6:63, Jesus said that God's Word is Spirit. To have God's Word in our minds is to be spiritually-minded. When I say "God's Word", I am referring to any train of thought that is in agreement with God's Word, not just verbatim verses from the Bible. Being spiritually-minded gives life. The word "life" here refers to life that comes from God in the highest order. The word "peace" refers to all things that come from that life, such as divine health, healing, deliverance, protection, preservation and prosperity.

Philippians 3:15 says, "Let us therefore, as many as be perfect, be thus minded..." The word "let" clearly indicates that the decision is ours. God loves humanity so much. Above all, He wants to fill our lives with His goodness, kindness and peace. He wants to give us a life that is superior in fulfillment beyond our imagination.

This kind of life is divine, supernatural and spiritual, and comes to us from God, Himself. God is a gentleman in the highest order of the word, and He will not force His love on us. He has to have our desiring permission. If we will initiate God's Word in our mind, He will show up to discuss the matter with us. He will then be there to show you how it will enhance your life, and how to cause perfection or maturity in every area of life. However, you must initiate the process. If you want perfection and maturity in your life, be thus minded. This starts with and through our minds.

Proverbs 23:7 says, "For as one thinketh in his heart, so is he..." First you think, and then you become what you've been thinking. If we are not pleased with what we have, what we can do, and who we are, we must change our thinking patterns. We are, today, because of how we have thought in the past. Since God's Word will not return void, this doctrine works for a non-Christian, as well.

God allowed His anointing to be manifested through many non-Christians in the Old Testament, as there were no Christians until the New Testament. If the occasion is Scripturally right, God's power will be activated. How much more ought we as Christians use this doctrine to be blessed and to be a blessing? The power of God has its birthplace in the available human mind.

In Psalm 119:88, the Scriptures say that a quickening (giving of life, a nourishing up, a preservation, a recovering, a replacing) takes place *after* the discovery of God's loving-kindness. God is the same yesterday, today and forever, and He has and always will be full of loving-kindness, goodness and mercy. Since God is that way, the *after* has to be up to humanity.

We first discover God's loving-kindness though a process of mentally finding it out, and then meditating and thinking upon the discovery. We, then, accept this truth deep own into our spirits, by talking and acting like it is true.

As a result, a quickening will take place. I have never been able to get anyone healed who did not believe in healing. Neither could Jesus. Believing begins in the mind. Quickening begins in the mind. That is why the Scriptures say not to be conformed to this world, but to be transformed by reading and thinking in line with the Holy Scriptures and Scriptural principles (see Romans 12:1-2, James 1:21). If we will do this, we can know the good will, the acceptable will and the perfect will of God. If we do not read His will and accept it as true, we will not know it.

In Romans 12, the word "transformed" is the exact root word for "transfigured" in Mark 9:2-3.[3] This is where Jesus went up to the mountain to pray, and upon returning, He was transfigured before His disciples' very eyes. When this happened, His clothing, as well as, His countenance glistened exceeding white. According to God's Word, this same thing happens to us as we renew our minds with the Word of God. When we start thinking like this, we start believing that we can release God's anointing, just like Jesus did.

Start believing that as He is, so are you in this world (see I John 4:17). Start believing that the Word of God is true, and that you will accomplish the works of Jesus and even greater works according to John 14:12-14. Start believing that Habakkuk 3:4 refers to you, "For as He is, so are we in this world....and His (or your) brightness (brilliant, clear, shining light) is the light (illumination of lighting, bright and clear, as the morning sun); He (or the ones that know they are as He is) has horns coming out of his hands: (rays of sunlight splendor that streamed or stream from them) and there is the hiding place of His (your) power." Keep in mind, that in the midst of that sunlight splendor is the hiding place of God's power and reputation.

In Matthew 18:3, Jesus said that we have to become as little children, before we can enter the kingdom of God. The kingdom of God is part of what Jesus paid for with His life. Study verses that refer to the kingdom of God and the kingdom of Heaven, and you will find that God wants us to

---

[3] Strong, James. *Strong's Exhaustive Concordance.* Massachusetts: Hendrickson Publishers, pg. 1072.

have life just the way He has it. This is typical of a good father. That is the reason Jesus said to pray that His kingdom would come and be on this earth just like it is in Heaven (see Matthew 6:7-13). According to Scripture, we must accept these things as a child would accept them, or we will not enter into this type of a lifestyle.

# IF THE DOOR IS CLOSED, THERE IS NO ENTRANCE

If we are close-minded, there is no instrument for God's power to work through, since our minds are the doorway to our spirits and to our physical lives.

In 1993, I held a Signs and Wonders crusade in Monterey, Mexico, in which I plainly saw this truth. There were several miracles taking place. Each day, I would preach 2-3 times in different settings, as well as, in different locations. Each evening, I would preach and minister Signs and Wonders in a centralized location under a tent that would accommodate 1,000 people. Everyday, there were many healings, miracles and even a few Signs and Wonders. It was very evident that God's power was present to do great things, and that I was proficient in releasing God's anointing.

There was one lady, who was extremely deformed from birth, with one leg more than four inches shorter than the other. Instantly, God's anointing caused her body to be straightened, and her short leg grew perfectly straight in front of approximately 1,000 people. There were 15 Americans who went with us and can also testify to these miracles.

I had an interpreter with me during the crusade, and I would have him to instruct the people on how to receive the anointing. When the interpreter was able to explain this to the people, they received some degree of instant manifestation, even to the degree of blinded eyes opening and paralyzed children walking. Their faces streamed with tears of thankfulness for God's goodness.

There were times, however, that the interpreter was also busy ministering to people, so I was left to try to communicate with the people, myself. I would try to understand their need through the language barrier. I would also try to explain to them how to receive. Almost every time there was no sign of relief or outward manifestation. Many times, I would try again and again to no avail. They could not understand English, as I could not understand Spanish.

The Holy Spirit began to talk to me and tell me what I already knew, but the message was now stronger in confirmation. Quickening comes after they receive the anointing in their minds. When I would get an interpreter, it was amazing how they would receive the anointing with manifestation. Several phenomenal miracles took place when I had interpreters. I have said all of this to say, when I could not communicate with the minds of the people in need of a miracle, there was little or no anointing received, even though I knew I was releasing the anointing to the same degree and many times even to a stronger degree.

With that said, I still believe that God is a good and fair God, and that there is much Scripture to support the fact that if a person is in a situation in which there is a communication problem, God can come to the level that is needed, and there will be an absolute blessing.

# ACCORDING TO OUR THINKING

Ephesians 3:20 says, "Now unto Him (God) that is able to do exceeding abundantly above all that we ask and think according to the power (God's anointing) that worketh in us."

I Thessalonians 2:13 tells us that it is the Word of God that effectually works in those who believe. What you believe is what you think.

According to Romans 1:16, God's Word is His power, and His power is His anointing. So, God can only do according to His Word that is working in our thoughts. Words work primarily through our thinking process. If we are not thinking God's Words, then His words are not working in us. It is easy to understand that there will be no working of God's Word in us, if It is not in our minds. God's Word is working in us, if we are doing the Word with natural actions. However, before a human can do anything naturally, they must think about it. We will never ask or even speak, until the thinking process has been active in our minds. If we do not think in agreement with God's Word, we shut the door to the anointing of God working in and through us. God is limited and has no liberty for His power to work in and for us.

Proverbs 29:18 says, "Where there is no vision, the people perish: but he that keeps God's Words, happy is he." The word "vision" in this passage is the Hebrew word for *khaw zaw*, which means to mentally perceive, contemplate with pleasure, especially to have a vision of, to provide a dream, to dream mentally, to have a dream habit, mentally dream a revelation or an oracle, or to bind firmly.[4]

The people who keep (attend and take) the Word of God are happy. There are two categories of people referred to in that verse. The first category of people are those who do not have visions as described, and they perish. The second category of people are those who mentally see God's Word as truth, to the point that is gives them pleasure. They quite often decide to have a vision; it is something they do on purpose, as a habit. With their minds, they provide a mental dream as seeing God's Word. To them it is a thrill, much like a child who daydreams about the impossible being possible.

Jesus said that whatever you bind on this earth, God would bind in heaven (see Matthew 18:18). People who have visions, never have the anointing and the power of God perish from them. In like manner, health, healing, happiness, prosperity and any other good thing never perish from them. They see the sunlight splendor of God's power leaving their hands, going into bodies and causing cures, recreations and Signs and Wonders, as they refuse to believe any other source.

I Corinthians 15:2 tells us that if we keep in memory (which is the mental realm), then we are saved. As we choose to think on God's Word, salvation (healing, health, prosperity, deliverance, wholeness) becomes a reality to us. Those who refuse to yield, experience continual loss of the blessings of salvation that God has freely given to all of humanity.

It is like a person who has a very wealthy relative who passes away, leaving a will, which provides them with great

---

[4] Strong, James. *Strong's Exhaustive Concordance.* Massachusetts: Hendrickson Publishers, pg. 1099.

sums of wealth. As they read the will and follow the directions for making the withdrawals, they are financially blessed. And if one day, they forget where the will is located and forget how to use it, they will experience a great loss. In like manner, what an even greater loss, when humanity does not activate all God has freely given them.

Philippians 4:8 ends with, "...think on these things." Let us look at what we are to think on, and why we are to think on these things. In verse 8, the Bible gives us a long list of things that we are to think on, "....things that are true, honest, just, pure, lovely, of good report, if there be any virtue (spiritual strength), of there be any praise..."

There is no knowledge upon the face of the earth that is more positive than God's Word. When we think on Scriptures or trains of thought that are in agreement with what Philippians 4 tells us, we become very positive-minded people.

Verse 7 gives us the reason why we should only allow things that are in agreement with verse 8 to be in our minds, "The peace of God which passeth all understanding shall keep your hearts (your spirits) and minds."

If we keep the doorway of our minds open only to trains of thought that have been filtered through Christ Jesus and the Word of God, we will have peace that comes from God, that passes all understanding. The doorway for God's anointing is the mind.

Not long ago, a television show came on in which professionals were analyzing a particular group of people throughout the United States. The group being analyzed was referred to as the "centenarians". According to historical findings, the centenarians were a growing number of people who were living beyond 100 years of age. The study sought to find out the factors that attributed to their longevity.

The medical group who analyzed these centenarians was amazed to find that proper nutrition and exercise were not the leading attributing factors. Instead, positivity was the common factor. They refused to become depressed, even when a loved one passed away. They refused to allow discouragement remain in their minds. Upon asking a 115-year-old woman about her health, she replied that she had had severe heart problems about 50 years ago, but refused to let the problems overcome her. These centenarians were not invalids, instead, they were very active. One of the ladies even drove a racecar! There really wasn't any mention about God being their source, but God's principles work for anyone. Very clearly, the truth that God is no respecter of persons was prevalent.

The greatest natural blessing and principle that God has put into operation for the livelihood of humanity is *air*. We need air to stay alive; therefore, it is the most important thing that the natural person needs. Yet, God allows the blessings of air to be available to both saints and sinners. In fact, if a saint chooses to live in conditions where the air is very poor, and the sinner chooses to live where the air is the best available, the sinner will enjoy God's greatest natural resource more than the saint.

Principles and laws that are in agreement with God's Word are really God's laws. Although, there aren't verbatim verses to establish them by the user, God's laws will work, because His Word will not return void. If there are laws of God that will work for a sinner or an atheist, they will surely work for a Christian.

# REGENERATION COMES FROM YOUR MIND

Our minds act as the doorway whereby God's anointing can go into our spirits and regulate goodness in our natural lives. Keep the door shut to the devil and all that he has to offer. If it isn't good in every respect, then it is the devil's invitation to bring torment into your mind, spirit and life.

Ephesians 4:23 says, "And be renewed (regenerated) in the spirit of or by your mind." We are renewed and regenerated in our spirits by our minds. If we want supernatural regeneration, it has to start in our minds. Regeneration first takes place in the mind, and then in the spirit.

Ephesians 4:22 says, "...put away corrupt, deceitful, lust-filled conversation." Verse 25 says, "...put away lying and speak only the truth." Verse 29 says, "...let no corrupt communication proceed out of our mouths, but instead speak words that are good and edify and minister grace to the hearers." Verse 31 says, "...keep bitter speaking, wrath, anger, clamor, and evil speaking away from us." Verse 32 says, "...be kind, tender-hearted and forgiving toward one another."

A person's spirit is regenerated and renewed by speaking only Godly words. It is important to be cautious with our words, because they are a product or proof of what we think. Matthew 12:34 says, "...out of the abundance of the heart or spirit the mouth speaks (and we will have and be whatever we speak)."

Knowing that our minds feed our spirits, we should not think ungodly thoughts, so we will not speak ungodly words, and thus not have ungodly things in our life. We are

77

regenerated and renewed first, in our minds, second, in our spirits, and third, in our flesh. If we are not pleased with what we have in our flesh or the realm of the natural, we must make sure our spirits are fed the Word of God. If we have a discontented spirit, it is because we have allowed our minds to think on things that are ungodly. Shut the door of your mind to the devil, and he will not and cannot get into the rest of your life.

Proverbs 18:14 says, "The spirit of man (or woman) will sustain (make provision for, feed, provide substance for) his (or her) infirmity (sickness, disease, grief, sorrow, supplication, or prayer request)." If we need sickness and disease depleted and health produced, our spirits must be strong. Jesus said in Matthew 4:4, "Mankind cannot live by bread alone, but shall live by every word that proceeds out of the mouth of God." God only speaks His Word, and He is always speaking His Word to humanity. If we will allow His Word to be in our minds, it will cause us to have life the way God intended for us to have it, even to the degree of regenerating and renewing.

The most spiritual thing in existence is God, Who is a Spirit. God and His Word are interchangeable terms. Our spirits must have food to stay healthy, strong and alive. There is no better spiritual food than the Word of God. If we want those things that the Scriptures teaches us are ours, then we must keep our spirits strong, and remember that our minds feed our spirits.

Hebrews 10:16-17 says, "This is the covenant that I will make with them after those days, saith the Lord, I will put My laws into their hearts, and in their minds will I write them. And their sins and iniquities will I remember no more." Sin, wrongdoing, faults, failures, weaknesses and inadequacies are erased from our lives when God's Word is in our minds. The torments and sin of satan and his kingdom are destroyed by the power of God in our minds. No wonder the devil wants to occupy our minds with anything that keeps us from victory. Light and darkness cannot occupy the same space; good and evil cannot occupy the same space. This is quite possibly the major area in which satan is defeating the Church, today. (I discuss this in greater detail in my book entitled, *Understanding Your Worst Enemy*.)

# STAYING BLESSED

Isaiah 26:3 teaches that we are kept in perfect peace as our minds are stayed on the goodness of the Father. This means we live in a place where not even the worst evil force can defeat us. We are kept in a supernatural level that is full of happiness, favor, rest, financial prosperity, safety and health as our minds are stayed on the Word. However, this can only happen, when we keep our thoughts on God, and keep from thinking thoughts of doubt, defeat, foolishness, idleness, uselessness, vulgarity or ungodliness. Walking in this peace is knowing that everything that pertains to this life or the eternal life is entrusted to Him.

# LEARNING HOW TO RECEIVE

Many people do not enjoy all that God has for them, because they do not know how to receive. In fact, many enjoy very little, because they do not know how to receive from God. Jesus said in Mark 11:24, "Whatsoever things you desire ("desires" are not needs, but things that are excess) when you pray, believe you receive and then you shall have them." When you learn to believe that you receive, then you shall have. If you can learn to "have" in the mental and the spiritual realm, you will have in the physical realm.

# GOD IS GREATER THAN SATAN

Scripture teaches that it is easier to yield to God's power, holiness and anointing, than it is to yield to sin. Romans 6 talks about "yielding". Keep in mind that the word "yield" in these passages in the Greek means to be still and to reflex or relax. Webster's dictionary says that it means to give up to a superior power, to surrender or to submit. This full meaning of the word "yield" will help you to understand how to truly yield to God's awesome miracle-working power.

Learning to receive from God is about totally surrendering mind, body and spirit. As humans, we often understand things better if there is a natural illustration. This is how Jesus taught. In John 3, Jesus said that just as a person is born in the natural, so must they be born again or born of the spiritual.

When I minister the anointing of God to people, I teach them to receive it the same way that I received it from God. Jesus said in Matthew 10:7-8 that we have freely received the power to heal the sick, cleanse the lepers, raise the dead and cast out devils. If you cannot freely (in the Greek means gratuitously or totally unmerited) give, you did not completely receive it.

When I minister the anointing to people, I tell them to surrender, relax and yield their minds to only what I am telling them. I always speak things that are the verbatim words of God or in direct correlation with the Word of God. Many times people's minds are so busy, that they cannot receive from God.

God has put the law of sleep or rest in operation to bless the human race, and it will work for the saint and the sinner, alike, as God has no favorites. He loves all of humanity. He proved that He loved all, when He gave the greatest gift, His Son. With the blessing of rest, we all must obey the simple law of yielding, surrendering and relaxing our minds. If we do not, we will not enjoy the blessings of rest or sleep.

There have been many times that I have been unable to rest or sleep, because my mind was doing everything but surrendering. In like manner, people often miss the blessings of God, because they have not learned to relax their minds.

As mentioned before, everything God has for us starts in the mind. Romans 10:14 says, "How shall they call on Him in Whom they have not believed? And how shall they believe in Him of Whom they have not heard? And how shall they hear without a preacher?"

Believing is a process that starts in one's mind. Hearing is the manifestation of knowledge coming forth by reading or hearing someone speak. The information presented to the mind can come through a preacher or a speaker. A preacher is someone who gives information that is supernaturally spiritual. That information enters the minds of people.

81

The greatest miracle a person can ever receive is eternal life, which is a part of salvation. It comes from a mind that has heard and accepted the Word of God. Remember the full meaning of salvation, and you will be able to receive everything else it stands for, in the same way you receive the greatest part of salvation. The lesser parts of salvation, such as healing, wholeness and prosperity, are receive in the same way the greater, eternal part is received.

Romans 6:12 tells us not to let sin reign in our mortal bodies. The decision is ours. Verse 13 says, "Neither yield your members as instruments of unrighteousness unto sin: but yield yourselves unto God." It says to yield our members to righteousness. This is the second step to receiving God's anointing.

When you understand how to yield your physical members to God's holiness, you have taken a giant step towards yielding your person to God's power. If a person is in the middle of a lake and they cannot swim, they are in a situation in which all of their physical capabilities are limited. They will soon die. However, if someone who is an expert swimmer comes to their rescue, they must totally yield, relax, surrender and submit to the saving power.

When a person flexes their muscles to receive aid for something they need or want, the degree of their physical strength will determine the degree of the aid. If there is a weight beyond their physical strength, the best thing to do is to get out of the way, yield, relax, be still, surrender, submit and give up to a superior power. In fact, you could be greatly hindered by even trying to help out. If it is easier to yield to a natural source of help than it is to yield to God's strength, then human strength is greater than God's, and it isn't.

I Corinthians 1:25 says that the weakness of God is stronger than man's strength. 2 Corinthians 12:9-10 says, "God's strength is made perfect in our weakness." When we totally surrender our strength, God can manifest His own. Paul went on to say, "Glory comes from my infirmities (weaknesses), that the power of Christ might rest upon me. I take pleasure in my infirmities (weaknesses) for when I am weak then He is strong."

When Paul yielded to God, a supernatural ability (God's power) was manifested through Him. He simply received God's miracle-working power, by being still and relaxing in his mind and flesh.

When you minister God's supernatural anointing and cause your mind to be totally surrendered, giving God's Word or principles prominence, His anointing will begin in your mind. This is the first step towards the manifestation of a miracle. Then tell the person to whom you are ministering to do the same with their mind. Next, do the same with your body. Literally, relax your muscles, especially in those areas that need the manifestation of a miracle. Tell the person to whom you are ministering to do the same. Then command those areas to surrender and relax to the saving, superior power, which is God's anointing.

The gifts of the Word of knowledge and discerning of spirits will often come into operation while ministering in this fashion, because you have opened up and yielded to the realm of the Spirit. You may begin to feel, see, smell, taste and hear things that the person you are ministering to is experiencing.

In Romans 6, the Scripture plainly tells us that instead of yielding to sin, we can just as easily yield to righteousness

(God's holiness, or to be like God and have His very reputation). We can yield to being like God just as easily as we can yield to sin. In fact, we can yield to having God's reputation, His anointing, His righteousness, and His holiness easier than yielding to sin. If that weren't true, then satan would be greater than God, and he isn't. If one yields or gives in to sin, they have yielded or given in to satan, as sin and satan are synonymous terms.

Romans 6:19, "...for as you have yielded your members servants to uncleanness and to iniquity; even so now yield your members servants to righteousness unto holiness." Just as simply as we have yielded to sin, by the same simplicity, now, yield to holiness and righteousness (having the reputation of God).

The devil has fed the Church such lies that the Church has remained defeated when it comes to the ministry of Signs and Wonders. The devil will tell you that you cannot do the very works of Jesus, because you haven't been to Bible school, or you do not know the Scriptures well enough, or you do not pray enough, or you aren't holy enough, etc. The Scriptures say that just as we yielded to sin, with the same simplicity, now, yield to God's holiness. You will notice that there are no "sin schools" or "sin colleges", yet we have professional sinners. We do not need to go to Bible college to obtain the riches of God's holiness for ourselves. All we need to do is to yield to it, act like it and talk like it is true, because it is the highest truth in existence.

Hebrews 3 talks in clarity about God's people not being blessed, because they wouldn't yield to God's goodness. Verse 9 says that they tempted Him. Verse 10 says that they grieved Him. Verse 12 says that they had an evil heart of unbelief. Because of that, they departed themselves from the living God. Verse 17 says that God called their action sin.

In looking at Hebrews 3 and 4, the problem becomes clear. They would not surrender or relax in their ability that was in their minds and flesh. Verse 11 says that they did not enter into God's rest. If God made them surrender, yield or relax, then He would be a tyrant, yet He is a gentleman. He will not force Himself or His power upon anyone.

Keep in mind that the word "rest" in the Greek has a fuller meaning, which is to pause, to stop, come to an end, refrain, as a type of heaven or a saturation of rest. This means the same as relax, yield and surrender. Hebrews 4:1 says, "Let us have reverence that not a promise would be left out that would keep us from trusting the superior power of God." The decision is ours. Hebrews 4:3 says, "If you believe you will enter this rest..." Hebrews 4:6-7 says that God is limited if people will not first believe and receive into their minds. Hebrews 4:9 says that there is a rest for the people of God, and verse 10 says that in order to enter into this rest, we must cease (stop from your efforts, mentally and physically).

Hebrews 4:11 deals with the mental realm. To fall away from this rest is to become involved with unbelief. According to this passage, a person falls into unbelief because they did not learn to labor. The word "labor" in this passage means to be prompt, earnest or diligent in study. Being single-minded is a type of labor. You will often find that there is labor in studying, meditating or thinking on God's Word. It becomes an actual battle or fight. The devil (or one of his imps) will be there to try to get you to be double-minded, and it will be a fight to stay single-minded on the purposes of God and His Word. Once you learn that the Word defeats satan's greatest onslaught, the fight is good. You will win every time with a victory. Learn to enter into God's rest and His anointing.

# YIELDING OR RESISTING

We are either surrendering (yielding to God's anointing) or we are resisting God's anointing. In Matthew 12:30, Jesus said, "You are either for me or you are against me."

Romans 13:1-2 says, "Let every soul be subject (submitted, surrendered or yielded) to the higher power. For there is no power, but of God: the powers that be are ordained of God. Whosoever therefore resisteth the power, resisteth the ordinance of God..."

If we are not subject to surrendering and yielding, then we are resisting. Verse 1 says, "Let every soul (our souls are our minds) be subject (or submitted) to the higher power (of God)." The last phrase of verse 2 says, "They that resist (the power of God) shall receive to themselves damnation." We will receive either the power of God or the damnation of the devil. Receiving is a simple principle that is in operation, one way or another.

# THE GOODNESS BE YOURS

Psalm 19:14 says, "Let the words of my mouth, and the meditation of my heart, be acceptable in thy sight, O Lord, my Strength, and my Redeemer." First, it is understood from a sound Scriptural standpoint that God is every place all of the time. Second, the word "acceptable" means enjoyment, pleasure and delight. God has no greater pleasure than to know that we are blessed (see John 2:4 and Psalm 35:27).

God watches over His Words to perform them. God is with us at all times. He will only activate His Words, and He only wants good for us. This makes it easy, as well as, desirable to speak the Word of God from morning to night. God's greatest pleasure is for humanity to be blessed, and this happens through and by His Word spoken continually from our mouths.

# FOR THE HUNGRY

Having God's anointing working for and through you is very simple, but at the same time it is only for those who are serious. God will become as serious with you as you are with Him. The following Scriptures teach that being serious with God and receiving that seriousness back from Him, happens in a supernatural way. Jeremiah 29:13-14 says that you will find the Lord when you search with your whole heart. He will then work supernaturally for you.

Jeremiah 33:3 says, "Call (have a deep-rooted concern) to me (Him), and I will answer you and show you great and mighty things that you know not."

Matthew 5:6 says, "Blessed are they which do hunger and thirst after righteousness: for they shall be filled." When we hunger and thirst after God and His goodness (His anointing) as we hunger for air, water and food, we will be filled.

Hebrews 10:21-22 says to draw near to God with a true heart.

2 Chronicles 16:9 says, "For the eyes of the Lord run to and fro throughout the whole earth, to shew Himself strong in the behalf of them whose heart is perfect toward Him."

Isaiah 38:16 tells the story of Hezekiah praying with his whole heart. God heard him and answered his prayer within a matter of moments. It does not take long to make our hearts right or for God to answer.

In James 4:8 God says, "Draw nigh unto Me and I will draw nigh unto you." According to 2 Peter 1:3-4, God has already given us everything we could possibly need or desire. I will end this chapter with the following Scriptural statement: God has given all that He is going to give us, now it is our turn.

# CHAPTER 8

# DYING, SO JESUS CAN LIVE

If you truly want God to be magnified in this world and through your life, you will have to die to the flesh and intellect. You will have to eliminate selfishness, which desires only to please self. You must be willing to go where God calls, and be willing to eat, sleep, live and even clothe yourself with what that area has to offer. You will have to be humble in order to be exalted by God. Jesus said that you would have to take up your cross and follow Him. You will find that the cross we are to bear is to love the unlovable. This includes unlovable situations, conditions and people. You will experience untold satanic opposition and persecution from people you will have to learn to love.

In the early 1980's, John G. Lake's daughter and son-in-law, Wilfred and Gertrude Wright, came to the church that Donna and I pastor in order to work with us in a camp meeting. I asked if they would accept our invitation to stay in our home, as I had read everything I could get my hands on concerning John G. Lake for many years, and I wanted to know more information first-hand. I asked Gertrude to tell me the greatest remembrance she had of her father. I was not expecting her answer to be that he was a man acquainted with great tribulation.

God must be the ultimate contentment of your whole being. All desires, concerns of the flesh and mind must give in to the paramount concern, which is Christ being magnified in us by life or by death. If you want Jesus to live in your life, you will have to die to self. A dead man doesn't care what people say to him. He doesn't care what people think or do to him. A dead man has no fear, no pride and no lust.

Jesus says in Matthew 11:12, "...the kingdom of heaven suffereth violence and the violent take it by force." He is talking about a child of God getting violent with the kingdom of darkness, the first heaven. This is where satan's kingdom is found.

In a natural war, the greatest threat is an opponent who is not afraid to die. That person has died to all self-ambitions and has a superior motive – to give his life for a cause. In that person's mind, they are as good as dead, so there isn't anything the enemy can do to change his or her mind. They will accomplish the task at any cost, because they have nothing to lose.

There are several ways a person can die to self. In looking at several of these ways, keep in mind that there are God-ordained ways to die to self. Often people do not choose God's ways to die to self, because of selfishness. Subsequently, the person who knows God's way of dying to self and avoids it, comes to a place of great opposition form satan, because they possess knowledge, which threatens satan. This puts him on the attack, attempting to convince that person to forsake this knowledge.

# GET ANGRY

One way to die to self is to become angry with satan. A person in warfare becomes extremely violent and dead to self, when they see the vile destruction that has taken place to someone they dearly love. Just one visit to your local children's' hospital will be sure to get you angry at the devil, as you are forced to witness the vile destruction that he causes in these innocent little ones. We need to know that he is our enemy. When you see those precious children in pain and torment, your heart will be touched. When you understand it is satan who is the author of such horrible torment, a rage will arise in your heart and life. This rage can cause a person to die out to self to such a degree that they will storm the kingdom of darkness with great violence. If we, as believers, do nothing, satan will continue his hideous efforts.

There was a time in which I was so hurt and so angry at what satan had done to people whom I loved dearly, that I began to die to self. When this took place, I did experience a portion of God's glory. Since then, I continue to give my life for the destruction of satan's purposes and his kingdom.

To a great degree, I no longer care what the circumstances are. I do not care what people say about me. When there is a desperate, overwhelming desire to avenge the people you dearly love, no price is too large to pay. When satan's destruction comes to your household, you will become very serious with God. You won't care what anyone else thinks or says.

If we would live seriously with God, we wouldn't see the vile destruction in our households. In Luke 12:48, Jesus said, "To whom much is given, much is required." We must understand, that as never before, we are at war with satan.

If there isn't anyone else to do it, I will promote the most powerful settings of God's power for the destruction of satan's kingdom, and God will be magnified in my body, whether it be by life or death (see Philippians 1:20). My greatest prayer is that the Lord forsake me not until I have shown His strength, goodness, kindness, mercy, compassion and love unto this generation and His divine supernatural, spiritual, miracle-working power and Signs and Wonders to everyone who is to come, so that the world will have to say that there is a God with Whom no other god or religious teaching can compete. He has never forsaken me and never will.

# GET HUNGRY

Another way to die to self is to become hungry. In Matthew 5:6, Jesus said, "Blessed are they which do hunger and thirst after righteousness: for they shall be filled." If a person is very hungry in the natural, they can become quite violent in order to fulfill that need.

This reminds me of a story I once heard, in which a young man wanted to be a successful minister, so he went to the pastor of his church, who he felt was wise and successful. The young man shared his ambition with the pastor, and his pastor told him that if he wanted to pursue a successful life in the ministry, there were things that he would need to do.

The pastor asked the young man if they could meet the following morning at the lake, in order for him to teach these things. As requested, the next morning the young man showed up and was full of questions, but the older minister said, "Only be observant of this day and the things that I do and say." The pastor proceeded to walk out into the water until it was up to his chest, and then asked the young man to come join him. When the young man came out to him, the pastor put his hands on the young man's head, and proceeded to push his head under the water. The young man figured this must be a baptism and went along with it, until the pastor continued to hold his head under the water for quite some time beyond your typical baptism. The young man fought to try to get his head above water, yet the pastor persistently held his head under the water. He feared the pastor must be trying to kill him, so he began violently kicking and fighting, knowing that in just moments he could die if he didn't get air. Finally, after quite an intense struggle, the young man overcame the pastor and shot up out of the water, gasping for a much-needed breath of air. He yelled at the pastor, "Are you crazy? Were you trying to kill me?" The pastor looked at him intently and said, "When you want to be a successful minister as much as you wanted that air, nothing can stop you."

We need to be that hungry, if we want to see God be God. The reason we do not see God be God, as He was to Jesus, is simple. There are not many people as hungry for God and His Word as that young man was for the air. This is because people's lives are too full of other things.

If my wife and I would have allowed our children, when they were young, to eat junk food all day long, they would not have been hungry for dinner. In like manner, when it comes to spiritual food, adults have their lives full of carnal things, and there is no room for Godly things.

If a meal was set before them that would give them strength and cause them to be free from sickness and disease, it wouldn't make any difference. They are full, and there is no room for anything else.

People, today, are so full of television, recreation, excessive living, the cares of this world, or maybe some religious teaching that has been handed down through the years that there isn't any room for the things of God.

If we will starve out those things that are taking priority over the things of God, then we will hunger for the things of God. God will draw near to us, because we are drawing near to Him. Then, we will see God be God.

During the days of the Great Depression in the United States, people didn't worry about their car payment or house payment, because many of them lost those belongings. They didn't worry about watching television, because there was no television. They were not concerned about the many things that fill people's lives, today, because most of them had lost everything. This caused some to become desperate enough to need God's power to work for them. They studied the Word of God, and put it into practice for hours everyday. They had prayer meetings that lasted for weeks. One particular prayer meeting lasted almost three months. They saw God be God.

# BE UNAFRAID

Another way to die to self is to be so zealous for God that you lose all fear. I Kings 18 tells of a man by the name of Elijah who truly dies to himself, so that God would be magnified in his life, whether by life or by death.

God hearkened to the voice of Elijah and proved He was the only true God. In I Kings 18:21-24, Elijah said to the people, "How long are you going to have two opinions? (How long are you going to say that there are two Gods?) If the Lord be God let us follow Him, but if Baal be God let us worship and follow him. I am the only prophet of the Lord and there are 450 prophets of Baal. Let us take two bullocks; and let the prophets of Baal take one and cut it into pieces and lay it upon wood with no fire underneath it: and I will take the other and do the same. And let them call upon the name of their gods and I will call upon the name of my God and the God who answereth by fire, let Him be God. And all the people agreed."

Elijah was challenging the teachings that were contrary to the Scriptures. However, one thing was different during those days than in our world, today. In that day and time such a challenge would mean that the defeated opponent would be destroyed at the discretion of the winning party. If Elijah's God would have not shown up for him, the 450 men that he verbally challenged would have tortured him to death.

In verse 25, Elijah told them to choose the bullock that they wanted, and to put it upon their altar with no trickery of fire under the altar.

Just as false ministries today have to use deception for influence and self-gain, that same evil spirit from satan was also present in those times. Verse 26 says that they took the bullock, dressed it and started calling upon the name of Baal from morning until noon, saying, "O Baal, hear us." But there was no voice, no answer.

That makes me think of the times we are living in. There are some religious people, today, who have services in which the people cry out, "Oh God, hear us!" and nothing ever happens. Their prayers are not answered. Some have a god who answers sometimes, but not often. They say, 'It's probably not the Lord's will." There are so many, today, proclaiming that they have the right way, and that everyone else is wrong. I believe we should all get together and serve the God Who will answer supernaturally beyond all the other gods, as the One true God.

In the latter part of this verse, the prophets of Baal leaped upon the altar with hopes that their greater sincerity would finally bring an answer from their god.

There are many people who are very sincere, but they are sincerely wrong if they are out of contact with Scripture.

Verse 27 says that at about noon, Elijah began to mock them saying, "Cry aloud, a little louder because your god is talking or maybe running around with business, or maybe he is on a journey, or maybe he is asleep and you need to awaken him."

You better believe that anger was kindling in the hearts and minds of those 450 men. You can imagine their wishful thoughts of torturing Elijah, as soon as this was over.

Verse 28 tells that after Elijah antagonized them, they cried out louder and started cutting themselves with knives and lancets until the blood from their bodies gushed out upon them. No matter how we torment and sacrifice, personally, if it isn't in line with God's Word, there won't be an answer. If our prayers are not answered in an undeniable supernatural way, you are either praying to the wrong god, or you are out of context with Scripture. According to Jeremiah 1:12, God cannot watch over anything but His Word. Isaiah 55:11 says that His Word will not return void.

Verse 29 tells that there was still no answer for the false prophets. Elijah then announced that it was his turn. He was seriously unafraid. Either God is God, or life isn't worth living. Elijah proved he had already died to self. As I said earlier, a person who isn't afraid of death is the greatest threat to his enemy. This was evident with Elijah as he spoke out to the crowd saying, "It is my turn, now!"

In verses 30-33, Elijah prepared the altar and the sacrifice, going to great extremes to make certain there wouldn't be any doubt of deception. He wanted everyone to know that his God was the only true God, and that He is the God of no competition.

As never before, we need Elijahs, today, who will not be remotely associated with the spirits of deception and fear, and who will die out to self. If we totally die out to ourselves, stop caring what people are going to think, and forget about our reputations and believe God's Word for Signs and Wonders, than the world will know that there is only one true God.

Boldly, proclaim that you are doing what Jesus did. You are manifesting arms and legs with the power of God's love that the Father be glorified. Understand that if it does not happen, you are dead to self in many respects. You are dead in reputation, pride and maybe your flesh. You cannot kill a dead man or woman. If you die first, you will not have to die a second time.

You might go through 100 services in which you announce instant manifestations of arms and legs with no results to make sure you are dead to self, so that God can truly get all of the glory. Your reputation will have to die. You might have to go for quite some time with what seems to be a destroyed ministry, where others may not want to be associated with you, because you are "too extreme". Someday (depending on how quickly you can truly die to self), someone in need of a missing limb will look you up, and there will be a manifestation.

Verses 34-35 tell that Elijah wanted to make sure the sacrifice was saturated with water, so it was done three times until both the sacrifice and the trench around the altar were filled with water. Just as in the times of Elijah, there needs to be a vast difference between the true miracle-workers of God and the deceivers. There needs to be such an extreme difference that the world can plainly see the difference. The extreme needs to be so severe that the deceiver will plainly know that our God is a God of no competition.

In verses 36-38, Elijah called upon God and fire came down from heaven and consumed the burnt sacrifice, the wood, the stones, the dust, and licked up the water in the trench! Verse 39 says, "And when all the people saw it, they fell on their faces and said, 'The Lord He is the God; the Lord He is the God'."

I am so angry at the devil and his lies that find their way out of even the mouths of Christians. Lies such as, "Don't seek for Signs and Wonders, because you know that the

Bible says in the last days people will be seeking Signs and Wonders." The true Church of the Lord Jesus Christ never *needs* any type of a Sign or a Wonder. We do not *need* any type of a supernatural manifestation. We have the greatest supernatural manifestation in all of existence – we will live forever.

We have been born again and are the children of a divinely supernatural God. We are partakers of His divine nature. The world is confused. They don't know which god is God. So, when they start looking for Signs and Wonders, we can give them Signs that will direct them to the true God, just as Elijah did.

When I am saturated with God's Word, I am not afraid of getting into error. I am not the least bit afraid of satan or hell, instead it's quite the contrary. The Scriptures teach that the devil runs to and fro over the whole earth. The reason he runs is because many, including myself, are chasing him. Each time we catch him, there is a good fight and we win.

## DON'T COMPROMISE

Another way to die to one's self is to not compromise. Daniel 3 tells the great story of three men who were dead to self. They would not compromise the Word of God even to the degree that they were thrown into a fiery furnace heated seven times hotter than ever before. That is where they saw Jesus.

God's grace is sufficient. It is in the great trials of life that you literally see Jesus. If you've never seen Him, don't get mad at others, because they have and do. Just start declaring God's Word as truth to the degree that your life depends upon it, and the devil will show up, and that's right where you want him. Now, chase him with words and actions that say you believe God's Word is true to the extent that you will die if His Word isn't true.

You will feel the heat of great persecution, and that will be fine, because your feelings have nothing to do with it. The devil is a god who works and maneuvers in the sense's realm. He wants you to focus your attention upon your feelings, to the degree that you will stop considering God's Word as the highest order of truth. If you give in to his lies, you won't see Jesus or experience the Signs and Wonders mentioned in the Scriptures.

In Daniel 3:27-29, not only did the three men literally see Jesus, but they were not harmed. There was not even the smell of smoke on their clothing. The best part was when the heathen king blessed the God of the three men and decreed that every people, nation and language must not speak a single word against God, which is and always will be the One and only Almighty.

In essence, God is the God of no competition. The world needs Signs, because they do not know which way to go. They are lost. Lost people need good, clear, positive signs for direction. Curse that lying devil who says you are seeking Signs. Signs follow you, because you are a believer. Jesus said, "These signs shall follow them that believe" (Mark 16:17-18). We need to come to the understanding as never before about what Signs and Wonders are, so that we can surrender to them. We need to know what the signs of a Christ-like person are, so that we can start behaving like one.

Joshua 10:11-14 tells the story about a man by the name of Joshua, who stood up in the literal sight of his countrymen and commanded the sun and the moon to stand still, so that God's people would be blessed. The sun and the moon stood still as God hearkened to the voice of a man who was dead to self.

We need to die to self to the degree that we will boldly stand before our nation and our communities, and declare that we are everything that God's Word says we are, and that we can do everything that God's Word says we can do.

I could give you many Scriptural examples of men and women who died to self, because they believed that they served a God that no other god could compete with, and Signs followed them. I want to challenge you to read the Scriptures, again, and find many of these examples.

# GET HUMBLE

Another way to die to one's self is to humble yourself.

I Corinthians 6:19-20 says, "...You are not your own. For you are bought with a price: therefore, glorify (have the same reputation that God, Himself, has) God in your body, and in your spirit, which are God's." Forget what you want, and start wanting what God's Word wants for you. Remember that a dead person has no wants of his or her own.

Do what you have to do in order to act and talk like God's Word is true. Go where you have to go, and eat what the people there eat. Sleep in the same conditions that they sleep in, and live like they live. Humble yourselves in the sight of God, and He will lift you up. Keep in mind that

God is everywhere, but if you cannot die to self where you are, go and do what you have to do, so that you may die to self.

# BE HOLY

In Isaiah 53:7, the Scripture tells that the worst accusations possible were blamed on Jesus, and yet, He did not open His mouth and attempt to justify Himself. A dead man will not try to justify himself, even when he is in the right.

In Titus 1:7, the Bible teaches that if we want to be used of God, we must be blameless, instead of self-willed. We must not be quickly angered, not given to wine, not to strike, and not given to filthy lucre (greedy gain). The Scriptures teach that if we are not self-willed, then we are blameless and unrebukable. If we are unrebukable, we are perfect, and according to Colossians 1:22-23, that is how God sees us.

In order for God's holy, pure anointing to flow through us, we have to be at least as holy and pure as the anointing, or we could not contain it. The only way to be as holy and pure as God, is to get our own abilities totally out of the way, and allow God's ability to work in us. God's ability is His grace, and God's grace can only work in a life that has no working or meriting actions. A dead-to-self person is the perfect criteria.

# RENEW YOUR MIND

Another way to die to self is to renew your mind. Romans 12:1, "I beseech you therefore, brethren (Christians), by the mercies of God, that you present your bodies a living sacrifice, holy acceptable unto God, which is your reasonable service." If we will die to self, making us holy and acceptable to God for a divine work, we can go on to the next step of being transformed (which is the same word "transfigured" in Mark 9:2, where Jesus' raiment and person became exceeding white as snow) by the renewing of our minds.

The renewing of the mind in this text is in agreement with the rest of the Scriptures, concerning this doctrine of renewing the mind with God's Word. The latter part of the verse says, "That you might prove or know what is the good, the acceptable and the perfect will of God." The highest order of God's will in existence is His Word. If we do not read it, we will not know the good, acceptable or perfect will of God. If we do not know the Word of God and He speaks to us, we won't know if it was God, the devil or our minds speaking. Hosea 4:6 says, "God's people are destroyed for a lack of knowledge."

If we will first die to self and then renew our minds, we will know how we are supposed to think, talk and act. We will become holy, as God is holy, and do the works of Jesus. In I Corinthians 15:31, the Apostle Paul said, "...I die daily."

# YOUR WEAKNESS IS GOD'S STRENGTH

In 2 Corinthians 12:9,10, God says, "...My grace is sufficient for thee, for my strength is made perfect in weakness." When we allow all of our abilities to die to self, the self is rendered totally useless or weak. We get out of the way, so that God's grace and power can be perfected.

I glory in my infirmities or weaknesses that the power of God may rest upon me. I take pleasure in infirmities or weaknesses, for when I am weak, I am strong. "Weak" means helpless, because I have died to my ambitions, desires and abilities. When you can die out to self in this fashion, you will have the strength of God perfected in and for you, that the Father may be glorified in His Son.

In Luke 9:62, Jesus said, "No man, having put their hand to the plough (start out wanting to have the supernatural lifestyle and ministry) and looks back, is not fit for the Kingdom of God." This type of person will not fit into this lifestyle. Just as the author of a jigsaw puzzle has an image that he wants to project, every piece must fit exactly for this image to be present. In like manner, Jesus was saying that our Heavenly Father has an image of a lifestyle and ministry that He wants presented to this world. We cannot consider anything that would distract us from following the Word of God. If we do, we will not fit into the image that God has for us.

In Luke 9, Jesus taught the people not to consider anything else but His Word. In verses 1-3, Jesus told His disciples to take the very miracle-working power of God and have everything on this earth just as it is in Heaven. He told them to go out and take nothing for their journey. Instead, they were to go and act as if God would take care of them, as much as He cares for the birds of the air. They did just that and experienced the Kingdom of Heaven's principles. They did not consider anything else.

In verse 13, Jesus told the disciples to feed the multitude with just a little boy's lunch. He told them that if they wanted to fit into the Kingdom of God, they would have to act like the Word of God is true, even in the most impossible situations.

If you can figure it out, work it out or accomplish it on your own efforts, then God would probably never even ask you to do it. In the Scriptures, God always asked people to do the thing that they could not do on their own.

In verses 23-24, Jesus told them to take up their cross and follow Him. The cross symbolizes dying to self. In verses 57-62, Jesus heard many excuses, such as, "Let me go bury my father first, and then tell everyone good-bye, and then I'll follow the Word of God." It does not matter what the issue is, we cannot let anything distract us from following the Word of God.

In Philippians 3:10, Paul said that he wanted to know Christ and the power of His resurrection. In verses 13-14, he tells how this can be accomplished. We cannot count self. We must forget all of the past and focus all of our energies on the prize. As many as are perfect or mature spiritually, live this way. If you want to be perfect or spiritually mature, be thus minded.

# CLOSING

I pray that this book helps to mature the Body of Christ to the point in which the works of Christ are manifested to the fullest, as spelled out in the Scriptures, and that the full work of Christ be completed, so that multitudes will be eternally changed, that we might go home.

*For information on other books or teaching tapes, write to:*

Mel Bond
Agape Church
140 N. Point Prairie
Wentzville, MO 63385
636-327-5632
*www.agapechurch.addr.com*